D0805868

THE FOUR SEASONS OF
the
House
of
Cerruti

THE FOUR SEASONS OF
the
House
of
Cerruti

Translated by Judith Spencer

COMPLETE REVISED TRANSLATION

Facts On File Publications
New York, New York • Bicester, England

The Four Seasons of the House of Cerruti

Copyright © 1983 by Arnoldo Mondadori Editore S.p.A.

English translation © 1984 Arnoldo Mondadori Editore S.p.A.

All rights reserved. No part of this book may be reproduced or utilized in any form or by any means, electronic or mechanical, including photocopying, recording or by any information storage and retrieval systems, without permission in writing from the Publisher.

Printed in Italy
10 9 8 7 6 5 4 3 2 1

Ellbochasim de Baldach, or Ibn Botlan, the doctor from Baghdad (XI century), in the teacher's chair, the illustration that accompanies the introduction of *Tacuinum sanitatis in medicina*. "Men," this learned man declares, "only want help from science. Not debates, but answers. It is therefore our intention in this book to shorten the lengthy discourses and present the essence of the different speeches."

The four seasons, the four elements, the four cardinal points—these orders in quartets governed the contemplations of medieval scholars, and shaped their insights into health and medicine, philosophy and literature, faith and emotion.

Now kept in the Oesterreichische Nationalbibliothek of Vienna, *The Four Seasons of the House of Cerruti* consists of just over two hundred illuminations, reproduced here in full, each one accompanied by a translated version of the original text. It is a valuable and moving document of daily life and of the way people thought—in a word, of the culture of northern Italy as it was exactly six hundred years ago. But both the illuminated illustrations and the text bring to life this medieval society, bound in matters of arts and science to the sage words of alchemists and herbalists, and peculiarly sophisticated even to twentieth century readers in its wisdom and insight.

The miniatures illustrate herbs, fruits from the orchard and garden, trees, field crops, wild and domesticated animals, and occasionally the preparation of these foods. All this is rendered in keeping with the actual style of life in the Po Valley at the end of the fourteenth century, a particularly rich cultural crossroads at the time, and one whose art is noticeably influenced by French and Bohemian borrowings.

Although critics attribute this manuscript to the artist Giovannino de Grassi, for his influence is certainly apparent in these pages, the illuminations are without doubt the work of many painters. These painters, while on the one hand observing contemporary reality and reproducing it according to the rhythmical flow of international Gothic style, also borrowed from illustrations from the Arabic tradition and from as far back as late antiquity.

The text is most certainly linked to this distant Arabic tradition. A figure on one of the first sheets of the manuscript, reproduced on page 4, depicts a learned man in his chair with two disciples. The manuscript calls him "Ellbochasim de Baldach." *De Baldach* means "from Baghdad." Ellbochasim is a corruption of an Arabic name. (In a more meticulous transcription than that offered in the Vienna manuscript, the name reads *A'bul Hasan al Muhtar ibn al Hasan ibn Abdun ibn Sa'dun ibn Botlan. Ibn* in Arabic means "son," and, in keeping with ancient Arabic usage, a person is referred to by giving his lineage for four generations.) Ibn Botlan, or Ellbochasim, was an Arab doctor who

studied in Baghdad, practiced in various countries within the Islamic world, was baptized a Christian with the name Giovanni, and died in a monastery in Antioch some time after 1068. His *Taqwim es-sihha* (Tables of Health) provide the material, knowledge, and ideas of *The Four Seasons of the House of Cerruti*. Ellbochasim's approach is related to the naturalistic philosophy of Empedocles and the medical biology of Hippocrates of Cos, who lived between the fifth and fourth centuries B.C.

According to Empedocles, the cosmos is comprised of four elements—earth, water, air, and fire. Placed at the four corners of a square, these elements provide among them the four fundamental qualities—heat from fire and air, moisture from air and water, cold from water and earth, and dryness from earth and fire. Everything in life has two of these qualities, each to a different degree. And there are four degrees.

In Hippocrates's biology, the four cosmic elements correspond to four bodily "humours"—air to blood; water to phlegm; earth to black bile, or melancholy; and fire to yellow bile, or choler. Health is the balance of these four humours. Illness is the disruption of this balance with a predominance of one of the humours. The treatment of illness consists of administering substances that balance the humour that causes the illness. The predominance of one humour also causes the variety in temperaments—sanguine, phlegmatic, melancholic (black bile), and choleric (yellow bile).

The four seasons, like Empedocles's cosmos and Hippocrates's biology, correspond to the four elements. The key, then, to reading *The Four Seasons of the House of Cerruti* is to be found in this series of quartets from which the positive and negative effects of every aspect of life supposedly can be deduced.

In this free but faithful treatment of Ellbochasim's work, the integrity of the text of the Vienna manuscript is preserved. It is a synthesis of the art of healthful living in which men have believed for more than two thousand years.

SPRING

I see when Spring is come
all the birds singing in the forest
and the saplings displaying a crest of green
and fish from their lairs out in shoals.

and maidens in the morn and evening
dancing with their lovers and making merry . . . .

Matteo Frescobaldi
Sonnet IV, lines 1–6

Spring commences with the vernal equinox when the sun enters the sign of Aries and ends when the sun has passed through Aries and the adjacent signs of Taurus and Gemini and reached the solstice. This is the time, as we know, when the days are longer, the weather is changeable, and vegetation and inclinations begin to bloom. The illustrator of this page of *The Four Seasons of the House of Cerruti* interprets spring by choosing from his repertory images of tiny birds on the branches of trees, espaliers of roses in bloom, young girls in flowing blue or pink dresses intent on weaving garlands. Other youths make crowns in merry groups.

It is a gracious and fond portrait. There is no hint of Virgil's *vere novo . . . incipiat jam tum mihi taurus aratro ingemere, et sulco attritus splendescere vomer*, "in the spring the bull has begun to bellow at the plough and the ploughshare gleams polished by the furrow" (*Georgics*, I, 43–46). In all of the manuscript's illustrations, in fact, a certain contemplative detachment prevails with regard to nature and work is portrayed as a joyous gathering of fruits or an exciting hunt. The text, on the other hand, makes no concessions to the Arcadian image. Ellbochasim, the wise man from Baghdad, has invoked divine assistance and proceeds with his discourse, as promised, in accordance with his well-balanced intention: *tota narratio nostra est iuxta moderatam intentionem nostram.* In his culture each of the seasons corresponds to one of the four elements: air, fire, earth, and water, which make up the cosmos. Spring "corresponds" to air, and because it is contiguous to fire and water, its nature partakes of the qualities of heat and moisture.

Like every other "object" included in the *Tacuinum*, spring is given seven categories of information. The first is its nature *(complexio)*; the second the modality or characteristics with which the object is to be preferred *(electio)*; the third and fourth are, respectively, the usefulness or harm that are derived from it *(iuvamentum, nocumentum)*; the fifth how harm can be got rid of *(remotio nocumenti)*; the sixth what is the result of its action *(quid generat)*; lastly, to whom, when, and where it is advantageous with regard to temperament and age, season of the year and region, according to the four cardinal points.

The information for spring is preserved here in the spirit of the original manuscript. We have already defined its nature; its middle period is preferable; it generally benefits animals and all that grows on the earth; it is harmful to watery bodies because it generates putrefaction. This harm is removed by purifying the body; it produces good humour and much blood in the body; it suits cold, dry, and temperate constitutions, young people and temperate regions.

Everything in creation has a suitable season for its use, depending on the opposition between the nature of the object and the season in question. Raisins, for example, which are warm and moist, are appropriate to the winter, which is cold and dry. This is the ancient medical principle of *contraria contrariis*. In grouping the objects by season, this curious theory was helpful in cases where the appropriate season was not immediately apparent.

THE WEST WIND
Ventus occidentalis

The wind that blows from the direction in which the sun sets is dry. The best is a wind that shows signs of veering northwards. Like the east wind, it suits moderate temperaments, people of all ages, in the spring, in the East, where it induces men to hunt along the cliffs with bow and arrow. Those who take to the sea for their trading greet it joyfully in the spring if they are bound for Laiazzo, Alexandria, or Acre in a galley. On land it activates the digestion, but causes shivering and cold. The remedy for this is warming by the fire and heavy clothes.

THE EAST WIND
Ventus orientalis

The wind that blows from the east is by nature moderately warm, and if it travels over meadows and rainy lands, it is useful because it kindles the spirits, *multiplicat spiritus*. People of every age with well-balanced temperaments can benefit from it, especially in eastern regions and when the sun enters the sign of Aries, Taurus, or Gemini. It is, however, painful to the eyes and nose and so avoid it on the face, chiefly when it causes gusty squalls and trees begin to bend threateningly. Use flower water to remedy the pain.

SAFFRON
Crochus

Bulbs must be dug up every fourth spring, kept in the granary, and replanted in the summer. The best saffron is the garden variety, the Chinese red type, but in the shops on the Rialto the Venetians sell the variety from Aquila. It delights the heart, cools the brain, and stimulates desire. But it induces nausea which is remedied with quince juice or a sharpish, aromatic wine. It is good for the blood, making it thin and pungent, especially in old people, and as Dioscorides, the Greek doctor and botanist and celebrated authority said, soaked in raisin wine it is useful against drunkenness.

VIOLETS
Viole

Keep in the garden violets that are the color of lapis lazuli; the little plants with many leaves are the best. When cooking them, boil lightly and briefly; the infusion makes a vinegar that is wonderfully effective against fevers accompanied by a parching thirst. The perfume of the violet calms fits; the drink purges bilious humours; violet water, obtained through distillation, is good for bodily pains in young children. By nature a little cold and moderately moist, the violet is suited to those with warm, dry temperaments and can therefore aggravate catarrhs brought on by harsh weather.

ROSES
Roxe

Roses make a joyous spectacle in the garden in springtime, but it is not only for this that they are cherished and admired. They are, in fact, beneficial to the heated brain, although they sometimes cause some heaviness and dulling of the olfactory senses. This can be remedied with either camphor or saffron. Fresh roses from Persia are the best. Ancient medical texts refer to six parts that are advantageous to one's health: the tip and the rest of the leaf, the pollen and stamen of the blossom, the tip of the stem and the rest of the stem. The nature of all roses is cold and extremely dry.

THE LILY
Lilia

The Greeks called the lily *leirion*; its ointment is effective in soothing the nerves. The best lilies are the ones with blue flowers which dissolve the superfluities of the brain, but they cause a headache which can be treated with camphor. The bulb, chopped with honey, protects the skin and makes the face beautiful; ground in a mortar with matured pork fat and applied to the feet for three days, it draws out the hard centers of corns. The water distilled from the flowers, if drunk frequently, helps women in childbirth.

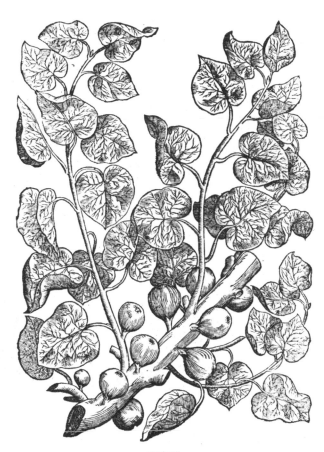

SYCOMORUS

THE SYCAMORE
Sicomuri

Similar to our mulberry tree, as was observed by Theophrastus the
botanist, the sycamore fig, or sycamore, bears sweet-flavored fruit
with pulp similar to that of the true fig. The best fruit is large and
black and beneficial to *apostematibus gule*, ulcerations of the throat.
They can cause stomachaches, rapidly becoming an undesirable food,
and produce unclean blood. In the spring, before the fruit appears, a sap is obtained from the bark by beating it with a stone.
Collected, dried, and diluted in water, the sap has softening properties for wounds and will bring difficult boils to a head.

RAINWATER
Aqua pluvialis

Rainwater is superior to any other kind: very clear, pure, light, and tasteless. The best rainwater falls gently in a good season. Second in preference is the kind that falls to the accompanying sounds of thunder. Avoid the sort that erupts furiously from sudden clouds with deafening thunder, lightning, and hailstorms. Beware of rainwater collected in cisterns as it combines a mixture of water that has fallen in different circumstances including melted snow, often in a state of putrefaction. Rainwater is beneficial for coughs, but causes hoarseness if impure. It always produces perspiration.

ALUM WATER
Aqua aliminoxa

It is known for its powerful astringent quality; therefore choose one that has this property in moderation and is pleasant to drink. It fortifies stomachs that are prone to vomiting; it eases childbirth for women with a tendency to premature births; it cures ulcers of the bladder. Used as a mouthwash, it soothes swollen gums. To cure external ulcers, use this water to bathe in. It partakes of the dry and is harmful because it is drying to the body. This effect can be treated with things that have intrinsic moisture and with sweet wine.

14

SUGAR
Cucharum

Ask the grocer for refined sugar which is hard, white as salt, and brittle. It has a cleansing effect on the body and benefits the chest, kidneys, and bladder. It causes thirst and stimulates the bilious humours, which can be remedied with unripe pomegranates. It is good for the blood and therefore suitable for every temperament, age, season, and place. Artificially white, it is very effective for tightness in the chest and when the tongue is unusually dry.

CANE SUGAR
Cana melle

In the fifteenth book of his *Geography*, Strabo writes that the sugar canes of India produce honey without bees. It is a local industry: they cut up the canes, cook and press them, and condense the liquor extracted from the pith by heating. The sugar should be very sweet. It is good for the chest, for coughs, and hoarseness; it benefits the lungs, purifying them wherever there is moisture; *urinam provocat*. It is good for the blood and is suitable for old people, but inconveniently *generat ventositatem*, which can be dealt with simply by washing it with water.

BRAN BREAD
Panis de simila, id est panis albus

This is made from *anima frumenti*, or the grain kernel. It must be well cooked with the expertise of a baker until it becomes a yellow or golden color. It is fattening, very nourishing, and suitable for people of all ages, at all times of the year, in every sort of region. The only inconvenience is not the obesity, which is a sign of prosperous well-being, but the *oppilationes*, or constipation of the stomach that can occur if you have bought poorly or, worse, hastily prepared bread that has not risen for the correct amount of time.

BLACK BREAD
Panis opus

Black bread is also nourishing and suitable for everyone. Choose the kind that does not have an excessive amount of bran and has been left to prove the night before baking. It is good for the stomach, but causes itching and scabies, disadvantages that can be avoided by serving the bread with fatty and oily foods. One must always take into account the size of the oven, which has to be in proportion to the amount of bread being baked. A small amount of bread in a large oven will be dry or burnt; too much in a small oven will not bake properly. The heat should be moderate: too hot will burn the outside and leave the inside underdone.

BROAD BEANS
Faba

Broad beans grow in the garden; choose ones with pods that are shiny, light-colored, and whole. They are beneficial for treating insomnia and headaches. By seasoning them with salt and oregano you can prevent that feeling of torpor which is the disadvantage of this food. Dioscorides maintains that beans are difficult to digest and for this reason cause fearful dreams, but he also says that cooked with water and vinegar and eaten unshelled, they stanch dysentery. Others believe that bean flour has the property of cleansing the skin and should therefore be used in the bath.

FABA

INULIN

Inula

ASPARAGUS

Spargus

This plant has large leaves, a hairy stalk, and yellow flowers similar to the chrysanthemum. Julia Augusta, it is reported, used to eat them every day. They cure occlusions, benefit the heart, and cleanse the chest of heavy fluids. Sugar, almond oil, vinegar, and salt can be used to eliminate the disadvantages of this plant: headaches and weakening of the blood. It heats the blood, which is not good. Chewed on an empty stomach, provided it has not touched the ground after it has been picked, inulin strengthens loose teeth. In Germany they make a potion from the roots, which is named after the apostle Paul and greatly improves the vision.

Pick those young stalks whose tips point downwards. They open up occlusions which prevent the humours from flowing regularly through the body's passages, and they stimulate carnal relations. Asparagus, however, is harmful to the intestinal hairs unless it is first boiled in salted water with vinegar. It is a nourishing food and very suitable for old people. Avicenna, the learned Persian savant, said that it imparts a pleasing smell to the whole body, and Dioscorides believed that carrying the roots on one's person or drinking its brew caused sterility in both men and women.

PARSLEY
Petrosillum

Galen, the very great Greek doctor, once said that parsley, one of the best known of all the garden herbs, is pleasing to the mouth and stomach. It is good for the health because it unblocks occlusions, helps the bladder to function properly, and relieves the discomfort of the female periods. It heats the blood and excessive use also causes headaches. The parsley from one's own garden is always preferable because one will never confuse it, from lack of experience, with other plants of similar appearance but of a different nature and sometimes, like hemlock, with deadly results.

ROCKET AND WATERCRESS
Eruca et nasturtium

The strong flavored varieties are to be preferred. They strengthen the blood and are suitable for old people and those with cold temperaments. They cause headaches which are remedied with a salad of prickly lettuce and vinegar. Dioscorides said of rocket that eaten raw and abundantly in one's food, "it arouses desire." Cooked and served with a little sugar, rocket cures children's coughs. Others have written that three leaves of wild rocket picked with the left hand and eaten immediately will cure an overflow of bile. The seed, chopped and mixed with beef bile, whitens scars; as a liniment mixed with honey, it lightens freckles.

MANDRAKE
Fructus mandragore

The cursed plant of witches, the mandrake has large leaves, var-
iegated blooms, and a forked root like a woman's legs. To pull the
plant out carefully, dig the earth around it, but do not touch it either
with a metal tool or your hand. Tie a rope around the stalk and
the other end to the collar of a dog. Whistle to the dog and as he
comes towards you, he will pull out the plant. Choose the fruit with
the most pungent scent: the scent will cure a headache and combat
insomnia. The ointment derived from it is rubbed into the skin as
a cure for elephantiasis and Negro infections. However, *ebetat sen-
sus*, it stupefies the senses and makes one dull-witted. Use ivy berries as a remedy.

MANDRAGORA MAS.

20

PARTRIDGE EGGS
Ova perdicum

These are found in the nests that partridges make in moorland grass and have a warmer, more delicate nature than hen's eggs. They provide only moderate nourishment and are therefore suitable for adolescents and the very old, in the spring, and at the very most for someone recuperating from an illness. The best way to eat them, whether fried or boiled, is to see that they are removed from the fire while the center still quivers, before it has hardened. This is not suitable food for a hard-working person, who would have to reinforce it with a generous amount of red wine.

PARTRIDGES
Perdices

The flesh of the partridge is good for the blood, a delicate nourishment that is soon digested and suitable therefore for old and young alike, in the spring, and especially for convalescents. It is, on the other hand, harmful for persons doing heavy work and carrying heavy loads. If they wish to eat partridge, it should be cooked with slices of bread. Old partridge is tough and unappetizing and harmful to those with melancholic temperaments; hence, choose young ones and tenderize the old ones by hanging them in the stillness of the night. Partridge liver, eaten over a period of a year, is beneficial in curing epilepsy.

PHEASANTS
Faxani

Eating pheasant has the same effect in every respect as eating partridge, but the pheasant is preferable. Young, fat pheasants killed by hunters are the best. They are good for the blood, though the blood will be thin because they do not give solid nourishment; hence they are not suitable food for peasants or others who have to work hard. Like partridge, the remedy lies in cooking them with slices of bread. They are, nevertheless, fit for princes and fine gentlemen and will put weight on those who are emaciated and worn out, but excessive amounts would be dangerous.

CASTRATED ANIMALS
Animalia castrata

There are three grades of castrated animal to be considered in order of goodness: first is sheep, second is goat, and the third is ox. It is better to choose animals pastured on hills of sweet-smelling grasses. The flesh of castrated animals is always easy to digest, but it makes the stomach lax, which can be remedied with fruit juices and pomegranate wine. It must, however, be young meat as the muscles of old castrated animals become dry and lack sweetness and grace. Excellent dishes are: the broth, which helps to counter melancholy; the boiled meat with parsley; and the hindquarters roasted with rosemary and garlic, previously chopped and sautéed.

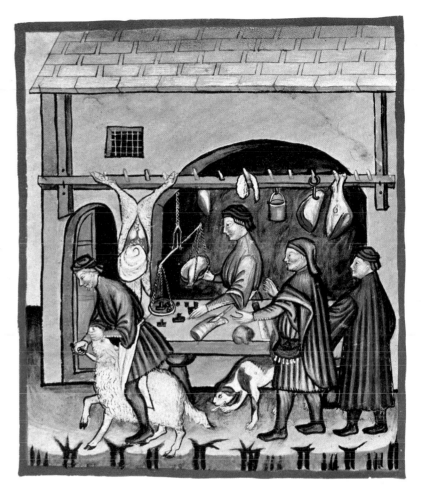

KID

Carnes caprarum et proprie edorum

When choosing kid at the butcher's look for rosy flesh tending to brown; also, a male of not more than six months, preferably an unweaned animal, is best. The meat of the kid is suitable for those with weak stomachs because it is easily and quickly digested; it provides excellent, almost perfectly balanced nourishment; but if it is salted, there is a risk of colic. And so sufferers from colic or epilepsy should not eat kid. They and elderly, enfeebled persons and those with cold, watery stomachs should, if anything, select the hindquarters, which are less moist than the forequarters, well roasted, and eaten with oranges.

MUTTON

Carnes arietum

With regard to mutton, fat sheep are preferable. The meat is good for the stomach and gives good rich nourishment despite the fact that some believe it has no value at all and should be banished from the table. Mutton is suitable for people with temperaments that are close to being well-balanced, for the young, and in the spring, but it is also true that the meat from newly born animals tends to be moist and phlegmatic. It is, and for good reason, unsuitable and even harmful for anyone who suffers habitually from nausea. Many find the smell offensive.

23

VEAL
Carnes vitulorum

According to Galen, and his opinion carries considerable authority, veal is better than mutton. It provides substantial nourishment and is suited to those with warm temperaments, the young, the springtime, and, regarding location, mainly southern areas. It is highly fortifying for those who exercise or work very hard. It is harmful to *spleneticis*, that is, those who are affected with spleen, but this can be remedied by movement and baths. Very young animals are always preferable and from mothers that have fed on excellent pastures. The meat should be cooked with chickens or fat capons and with parsley.

SALVIA MAIOR

FEET AND LEGS
Pedes et tibie

Lambs' and kids' feet and legs are the best and the forelegs more so than the hind ones. They are a good, substantial food for children and old people, in temperate regions, strengthening and spreading to wherever necessary in the body. They have other major qualities like healing bone fractures, easing hernias, providing nutritive viscous matter to tuberculosis sufferers. Take care, however, because they promote colic; to prevent this unpleasant effect, the housewife should see that they have been properly boiled, until the meat comes off the bone, and that they are served with vinegar and saffron to remove any harmful effects.

PRAWNS
Gambari

Only those prawns caught near good grassy shores where the water runs rapidly over rocks will appear on the wise man's table. They generate phlegmatic humour, but they have other merits: they induce sleep and help tuberculosis sufferers, particularly if cooked in milk. But they make the head feel heavy and this can be remedied by seasoning them with pepper and vinegar. The ashes obtained from burning the prawns and their shells are eaten or drunk together with gentian as a specific against a rabid dog bite.

CITRINE WINE
Vinum citrinum

Citrinum is the color of the citron. Citrine wine is a white wine that should be clear and a vintage wine. It generates acute bilious humours and protects against poisons, especially cold poisons. It is harmful in that it causes men to lose their desire for women, but the remedy for this is to serve the wine with sour quinces. Regarding wine, Dioscorides has written: all drunkenness is harmful, but there is an instance when drinking too much is useful and that is when a man has drunk only water for a considerable time. Then the wine will open the passages by which the superfluities of the senses are invisibly purged.

HONEY
Mel

There are many excellent qualities to be found in honey: it cleanses the chest and the stomach; it purges the abdomen; it keeps the humours of the flesh and the mouth from decaying. It heats the blood and is suited to those with cold, moist temperaments, and to the elderly. Its season is the winter, its region the mountains. The thirst that it causes and its transformation into bilious humour may be considered harmful, but the remedy for this is to serve it with sour apples. Winter honey is the worst, summer honey mediocre, and spring honey to be preferred; it should have a pure fragrance and be thick with a slightly reddish color.

SUMMER

And lemons, citrons, dates, and oranges,
  And all the fruits whose savour is most rare,
Shall shine within the shadow of your trees;
  And everyone shall be a lover there;
Until your life, so filled with courtesies,
  Throughout the world be counted debonair.

Folgore da San Gimignano
"Sonnets of the Months," VII, lines 9–14

Translation taken from *The Early Italian Poets*, D. G. Rossetti, Anvil Press Poetry, 1981.

The first of the six things essential to health, according to Ellbochasim, is the *praeparatio aeri*, or the correct adjustment of the air. When one of the qualities of the air is in excess, then the opposite quality must be modified artificially, if that does not occur naturally. If it is too hot in the summer, sprinkle the house with fresh water and vinegar and here and there arrange flowers, boughs, and sweet-smelling herbs, like violets and roses, reeds and willow leaves, boughs from the mastic tree. The house will be healthier, especially when the southerly winds blow, if it has a northern exposure and windows on all sides of the house for ventilation; that is, from east to west and from north to south. Rooms should be ventilated regularly or the air will become foul.

In the summer it is beneficial to stay occasionally in a country house. The countryside provides food for the city and, similarly, human life is prolonged by frequenting the countryside, whereas life is shortened by the idleness and business transactions of the city.

The learned Galen tells us that those who do not exercise in the summer, when the intense heat makes them terribly thirsty, should drink only spring water and guard against water from melted snow and artificially cooled wine. In our youth our bodies do not appear to be harmed in any way, but with increasing age and the damaging effects of certain practices, we incur diseases of the nervous system, the joints, and internal organs which are either incurable or very difficult to cure.

Early summer is the most beneficial time for the body when the sun is in Cancer. It dissolves the excesses that collect from the foods we eat and cures the cold illnesses; it increases the bilious humours and dry substances; it slows down the digestion; hence, one should choose a suitable diet to provide a contrast to the excess of bile.

In the summer some doctors advise carrying in one's hand a sponge soaked in rose water and rose vinegar, to be inhaled frequently, and sprinkling one's clothes with various distillations. The following recipe is an excellent example: four pounds of rose water, one of best-quality vinegar, two-thirds of an ounce of red roses, an eighth of an ounce of sandalwood, one-sixteenth of an ounce of camphor, and finally the very smallest quantity of musk, spices, and ambergris. Pound in a mortar the dry items, except for the spices, musk, and camphor; dissolve everything in the rose water, leave in an alembic for nine days, and, lastly, distill the preparation.

An afternoon nap should be avoided, but if unable to abstain, sleep on the long days in Cancer, on a leather chair and not on a soft bed, the head raised without inclining it either backwards or forwards, but to one side so that there is less evaporation from the brain.

CHERRIES
Cerosa dulcia

According to the evidence of Pliny, cherries did not exist in Italy until they were brought from Pontus by Lucullus after his victory over Mithridates. The best ones have firm flesh and have ripened in the sun on rocky soil. They loosen the belly, particularly the very sweet cherries, in spite of the fact that they are less useful to the stomach. They putrefy rapidly in the viscera; this can be avoided by eating only a modest amount, with a good, fragrant wine. If a large amount is eaten, drink water and abstain from other foods as cherries are rapidly digested and eliminated. They generate phlegmatic and bad blood.

BLACK CHERRIES
Cerosa acetosa

These are excellent dried and sugared. They quench the thirst of a high fever and stimulate the appetite; they are beneficial *bene acetose*, if very sour, in curing acute bilious attacks; they dry out the excesses of the stomach and settle it. They are very nourishing. The discomfort they cause to the teeth and nerves can be removed by combining the cherries with sweet almonds and raisins. The gum from black cherry and cherry trees, taken in watered wine, helps to cure old and tenacious coughs and clears and sharpens the eyesight. In plain wine it is a remedy for kidney stones.

APRICOTS
Armoniacha

Grisomilla, **id est armoniacha,** or Chrysomela or ermelin; the best apricots come from Armenia where they originated, as indicated by their Latin name, *Prunus armeniaca.* They generate phlegmatic blood and are used to provoke vomiting. Their nature is cold, they make the stomach cold, and they decay easily, in which case they must be eliminated with an emetic. Apricots are used to make an oil which is an effective cure for inflammations, ulcerous swellings, and impediments of the tongue. The oil is also useful in treating earaches.

MEDLARS
Nespula

Choose the plumpest ones. The nourishment they give is dry and suited to those with hot temperaments. They are a protection against drunkenness and are much appreciated by pregnant women as they stimulate the appetite and dispel nausea which is a common complaint. But they are harmful to the stomach and the digestion, which can be alleviated with brown sugar. Mix together some dry medlars with essence of roses, numerous cloves, a little red coral, and nutmeg which, applied to the mouth of the stomach, will effectively curb vomiting from food.

PLUMS
Brugna

Sufferers from bile should eat plums, because their principal benefit is to stimulate bilious fluid, generating watery humours. Sweet damascene or damson plums are the best, delicious-tasting especially when cooked in wine with the addition of rose sugar, which prevents their harmful action of binding the stomach. Water distilled from the flowers kills body worms. A decoction of the leaves in wine is made for gargling and rinsing the mouth; it is excellent for catarrh, the throat, the uvula and the gums.

PRUNUS

PEACHES
Persica

The tree comes from Persia and it is said that it was originally poisonous and that in Egypt the fruit became harmless, regenerated by the fine climate. The sweet-smelling, aromatic peaches are the best; they relieve high fevers generating a thin phlegm. The flowers loosen the body, cause perspiration and draw out water from dropsy sufferers. The kernels inside the peach stone are good for body pains. Pound them in a mortar and boil in vinegar to make a paste that, it is said, will make the hair grow. Six or seven of these kernels taken before drinking prevents drunkenness.

PEARS
Pira

Fragrant and perfectly ripened pears generate cold blood and are therefore suited to those with hot temperaments, in the summer, and in southern regions. They are salubrious for people with weak stomachs, but harmful to the production of bile. The harm can be remedied by chewing cloves of garlic after the meal. We find in Dioscorides, that most diligent writer, that a drink of pear wood, powdered and dissolved, is effective against poisonous mushrooms. Others believe that by cooking wild pears together with mushrooms, you will avoid any harmful effects.

33

SOUR APPLES
Mala acetosa

They produce cold, delicate nourishment and phlegmatic blood, and are suited to those with phlegmatic or bilious temperaments. The best sour apples come from Pontus in the opinion of the ancients. Their exceptional quality is in the treatment of syncopes, but they are harmful to the joints and nerves, which can be remedied with white wine. Some say that they cause loss of memory. In any case they taste better if cooked under the embers, sprinkled with sugar, and served with candied anise, or followed by rose or cinnamon sugar.

MELONS
Melones dulces

We are told by the Arab doctor Ellbochasim de Baldach that the best melons come from Samarkand. They should, in any case, be perfectly ripe, nourishing, brightly colored, and fragrant. They promote blood moderately and suit phlegmatic and bilious temperaments. They relieve the pain of calculi and cleanse the skin, but cause a flux from the belly, which can be treated with syrup of vinegar. Eat melon with mature cheese and salty foods and drink a fine wine, but not too strong; then eat some other nourishing food. This is a suitable food for when the weather is very hot.

WATERMELON
Melones insipidi

WATERMELONS FROM THE EAST
Melones indi et palestini

In Tuscany, where they are called *cocomero*, they are used to relieve parched throats during the heat of Leonis August. For a burning fever it is useful to hold some cold watermelon in the mouth. It provides modest, watery nourishment, but it gives protection against biliousness, and *provocat urinam*, is diuretic. However, watermelon can cause stomachaches, which can be eased by immediately eating other foods. Always choose really ripe watermelons, which are recognizable by the sound obtained by tapping the outside.

These melons, from India and Palestine, are large, sweet, and yellow. Like the true melon and watermelon, their nature is cold and moist, to a slightly higher degree than average. Choose large, very sweet, watery ones; they are good for illnesses caused by intense heat. They hinder digestion, which can be remedied with sugar or barley sugar. They produce only watery blood and, like the Italian watermelons, they are suited to those with hot temperaments, in the summer, and in southern countries.

PUMPKINS
Cucurbite

If you want extra large pumpkins in the garden, take a seed from the center of the fruit and place it in the ground with the tip facing downwards. Take care that women do not come near because if they touch the pumpkins, they will prevent them from growing; they should not even look at them if it is the time of their periods. Fresh pumpkins with green skins are the best. Their nourishment is cold and modest and they alleviate thirst. However, they purge the stomach quickly so that one must counteract their effect with salt water and mustard. Wine kept in a scooped-out pumpkin overnight and drunk calms the whole body.

AUBERGINES (EGGPLANT)
Melongiana

Fresh aubergines with sweet flesh are the best. They are useful in treating fluxes of blood in the vomit caused by a weakness of the stomach. The aubergine is harmful, however, because of its property of generating melancholic humours, which then increase in the head unless the aubergine is combined with oily substances that absorb the humours. They are suitable for old people, those with cold temperaments, the autumn, and northern countries. When picking aubergines, married women and virgins should be on their guard against aroused males, for the nature of the fruit is hot and moist and its melancholic odors induce deviations from decent behavior.

ALMONDS
Amigdale dulces

In the month of August, when the outer shell begins to crack, the almonds are knocked down from the trees. The large, sweet ones are the best and they have singular qualities: they overcome anxiety, remove freckles, and eaten before drinking, they prevent drunkenness. They stimulate the body's digestive humours, but are harmful to the intestine. An excellent remedy in this case is sugar mixed with poppies. Various texts advise that almonds should be ground in a mortar, combined with verbena water, and then applied to the temples with a bandage: this will relieve headaches and induce sleep.

AMYGDALAE

BASIL
Basilicum curatum

Various plants in the garden have this name and they all have a hot and dry nature, but in varying degrees. Choose leaves from the *curatum* with the sweetest perfume; it helps to dissolve the brain's superfluities and breeds strong blood, but *replet caput*, it fills the head; the water lily will provide the remedy.

BASIL OCYMUM
Ozimum citratum

Another kind of basil, called "ocymum," with smaller leaves and branches, whose perfume recalls the citron, has been much discussed and argued over by the authors. It was first thought that it should be avoided because goats instinctively rejected it. It was then proved that goats did eat it and that drunk with wine and a little vinegar, it cures scorpion bites. It may be recalled in this regard that Dioscorides noted that you will feel no pain from a scorpion's bite if on that day you have eaten basil. Nevertheless, it is astringent, the juice purges the intestine and generates strong swelling humours. It obscures the sight; the remedy is purslane.

CUCUMBERS
Cucumeres et citruli

Choose large ones from the garden that have not yet turned yellow. Their cold, moist nature helps reduce a burning fever. They are diuretic and produce watery blood, hardly laudable. They cause stomachaches and pains in the lumbar region which can be cured with honey and oil. Cut into slices and applied externally, they are very effective in reducing severe inflammations. We also learn from Dioscorides that cucumber juice mixed with the seeds and flour and dried in the sun cleanses and beautifies the complexion so effectively that young girls frequently use it.

CUCUMERES

GALINGALE
Galenga

Galingale is a wild rush with a penetrating odor and spicy flavor. It generates strong humours and is suited to those with cold, moist temperaments and old people. It can prove harmful to the heart and for this reason is taken with oily foods. Having a dry and extremely hot nature, it is prescribed for the sciatic nerve which, as we know, is impaired by the cold and dampness. Taken as snuff, it soothes the brain; held in the mouth, it removes any bad smells and it sweetens the breath. Chewed or taken as a potion, it acts as an aphrodisiac.

SAGE
Salvia

Its nature is hot and dry and it breeds thick and sometimes hot blood. It is good for the stomach and cold diseases of the nerves. The sage that grows in the kitchen garden is generally used, but greenwood sage is better for producing heat. Its digestion is slow, but it can be speeded up with a decoction of honey. We read that if a woman who has slept alone for four days drinks this and then has sexual relations, she will immediately become pregnant. To this end, women who survived the plague in one town in Egypt were made to drink the juice of sage leaves so that the town could quickly be repopulated.

40

HYSSOP
Ysopus

All the authors are agreed that no garden should be without hyssop so that one can have it at its best, fresh and homegrown. It is beneficial for a damp chest and coughs and is therefore good for those with cold and moist temperaments and old people, as well as the very old. It also has many other uses: applied with hot water it removes bruises resulting from blows; chopped with salt and cumin, it makes an effective poultice for poisonous snakebites; mixed with oil, it kills lice and relieves itching. But it does harm the brain because of *fumositate sua*, its smoky fumes which can be cleared with barley sugar.

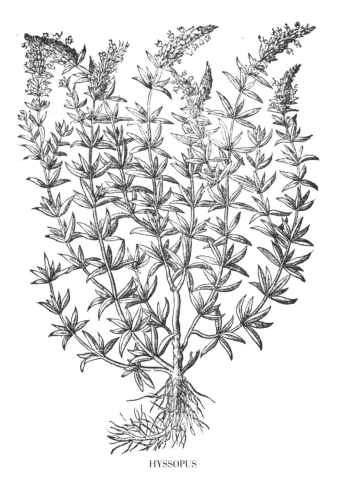

HYSSOPUS

ANISE
Anisum

It is chiefly the seeds of the anise plant that are used. They are slightly elongated in shape, joyously scented with a flavor that combines the sweet, the sharp, and the somewhat bitter. Anise is useful in many ways, but its digestion is slow; therefore, it should always be finely chopped or carefully chewed. Mixed with bread, it lends a pleasing, aromatic flavor; roasted together with mint, it helps the fluxes of the stomach; taken as a drink or smelled, it calms hiccups, induces sleep, and expels renal calculi. It removes obstructions from the body, is a diuretic, dispels flatulence in the stomach and intestines, and encourages the flow of milk in nursing mothers.

DILL
Aneti

Dill is usually sown in the garden so that it will mix with the other vegetables and give them more flavor. The tender, fresh, green plants are the best. It is particularly good for cold stomachs that tend to flatulence. It facilitates sleep and it is said that for this reason the ancients put it in garlands. It is harmful to the kidneys and may cause nausea, which can be treated with fraxinella. According to Dioscorides, its continual use in drinks has unfortunate effects on the eyesight and it also dries up the male sperm.

MINT
Menta

Small plants with thick leaves are preferable. It is good only when the stomach is in cold and moist temperaments, but it is not good if one has a hot stomach, due to its hot and dry nature, which heats the blood. Its scent is used to revive the spirts of someone who has fainted. Added to pomegranate wine, it cures hiccups and stops vomiting. The water obtained from distilling the whole plant (and the decoction should be quite strong) is a sure remedy, taken as a drink, for a bleeding nose. If mint leaves are put into milk they will stop it from coagulating.

MARJORAM
Maiorana

It is probably the delightful aroma of the marjoram plant that makes it so pleasing to women, nearly all of whom grow it and care for it diligently in the garden and in pots on the balcony or loggia. One has nothing but praise for it. It appears to be in no way harmful; rather it stimulates the blood and is good for cold and moist stomachs. If a small quantity of juice, distilled from marjoram, is placed in the ear, it will dispel any pain, as well as any whistling, and it is useful for deafness. Inhaled through the nose, it clears the head of phlegmatic humours and purifies and comforts the brain.

RUE
Ruta

WORMWOOD
Absintium

Ellbochasim, the scholar from Baghdad, states that the best wormwood comes from Pontus; it has smaller leaves and flowers than other wormwood plants and is pleasantly aromatic, not abominable-smelling like the others. He goes on to praise the so-called Roman wormwood which did not actually grow in the area around Rome or even in Italy, but in Bohemia, Hungary, and Transylvania. It helps cold stomachs, is good for obstructions of the liver, stimulates the appetite, and kills worms. It heats and thickens the blood, but is astringent. Its harmful effects can be remedied with sugar, vinegar, herbs, and almond oil.

This plant is an antidote for poisons and helps epileptics, yet it causes headaches. The best place to grow it is in the shade of a fig tree; a green, fresh plant is preferable. Its virtues as an antidote are well known by the weasel who, it is said, prepares itself with rue before it goes out snake-hunting. Some believe that it has powers against spirits, relying on a passage from Aristotle in which the Stagyrite discusses its fascinations or enchantments. But everyone knows, on Galen's authority, that rue "extinguishes the flames of Venus."

HOREHOUND
Marubium

Like dill, horehound should be used fresh from one's garden. This plant generates the humours and is suited to those with cold and phlegmatic temperaments. It is good for the stomach and for a damp chest, but is difficult to digest unless accompanied by cooked must, herbs, and vinegar. To treat an excess of bile, when pain is caused by obstruction of the body's passages, a very effective potion of horehound is made by boiling the leaves in strong white wine with roots of bugloss, inulin and eupatorium, rhubarb, and aloe wood. Boil the mixture until it is reduced by one-third and take it in the morning for ten days.

MARRUBIUM

PELLITORY OF SPAIN
Herba piretri

Fresh and tender, pellitory adds flavor to cold foods, but causes thirst and remains on the stomach for a long time; for this reason it is eaten with celery. The root, which is as thick as your thumb, long and pungent, is used to make an infusion, with vinegar, which serves as a mouthwash to relieve toothache. If chewed, the root stimulates the flow of phlegm; mixed with oil, it causes sweating and is an effective treatment for prolonged trembling as well as for paralytics.

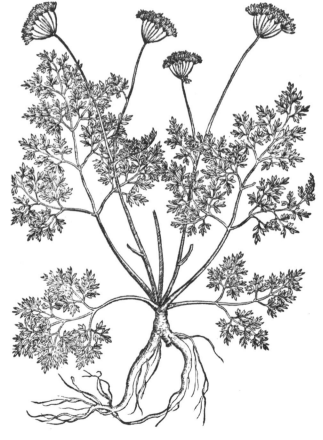

PYRETHRUM VERUM

MUSTARD
Sinapi

The seeds of the mustard plant are used to make the condiment, which is served with food and stimulates the appetite wonderfully. Because of its vaporous quality it sometimes penetrates the nose unpleasantly, rising to the brain and causing sneezing. Mustard, which thins the blood, is useful mainly against gout. It is also useful against sciatica if mixed with figs and applied to the affected area until it turns red due to the very hot nature of mustard. The harm that it may do to the brain can be avoided by preparing it with almonds and vinegar.

GARLIC
Alea

When picking garlic from the garden, select the *modice acuitatis*, moderately pungent. It generates thick, strong humours and is suited to those with cold temperaments, the elderly and very old, mountainous areas, and the north. It has many advantages. It is effective against cold poisons, scorpion and adder bites; it kills worms, clears the voice, and soothes chronic coughs. It can damage the eyes and brain and to prevent or remedy this, vinegar and oil are necessary. Pounded in a mortar with black olives, as the Greeks do, garlic is useful for dropsy sufferers.

MILK
Lac dulce

SOUR MILK
Lac acetosum

Milk provides us with *nutrimentum bonum*. It is suited to the summer, adolescents, and well-balanced temperaments. The best milk is supplied by the shepherds from their sheep, but not all the authors are agreed on this point. Some believe that goat's milk most closely approximates mother's milk, which, it is unanimously agreed, excels all others for its balanced ingredients; others prefer cow's milk. Milk is good for the chest and the lungs, but harmful if you are feverish or have a headache. You can remedy this with seedless raisins. Never drink wine on top of milk.

Sour milk is also suited to the summer, to young people and adolescents, those with balanced temperaments, and hot ones as well. It produces an excellent humour. The authors inform us that milk incorporates three substances: one is watery and called whey, and two are thick, of which one yields butter, the other cheese. Choose a *multi butyri* sour milk, one that abounds in the substance for making butter. Sour milk is excellent for quenching thirst, but harmful to the teeth and gums; hence it is a good idea, after drinking it, to gargle with mead.

FRESH CHEESE
Caseus recens

The thicker part of the milk condenses with the addition of rennet, the whey is expertly drawn off, and the cheese is formed. It is a very nourishing, substantial food which softens and fattens the body, but causes obstructions; therefore it is wise to eat cheese with walnuts or almonds. The more balanced the substances of the milk and the healthier the animal, the better the cheese will be. It is suited to those with hot temperaments, the summer and hot regions, but also, sometimes, to the winter or cold places for the reason that the cheese is digested better.

RICOTTA
Recocta

Ricotta is made from the whey of milk. It is nourishing and fattening and thickens the blood. It tends, however, to cause obstructions and is difficult to digest. It should be said, nevertheless, that in the opinion of Avicenna it is less harmful to the stomach than fresh cheese. To avoid the above-mentioned harmful effect, it should be eaten with butter and honey. Ricotta is a food for those with hot temperaments and robust, young people; it is good at the beginning of the summer and in the mountains. The best ricotta is made from pure milk; the salted kind, which is eaten in Lombardy, has little nourishment and makes you thirsty.

JUNKET
Lac coagulatum

Junket is coagulated milk which got its name from the reed baskets (*giunco* in Italian) in which it was put to drain. The best junket is made from the milk of young animals and makes the blood phlegmatic. It is useful in treating swelling of the stomach, but it lies heavily on the stomach and is therefore more suitable for robust, young people with hot temperaments. In any case eat it infrequently, at breakfast, sprinkled with sugar or a pinch of salt to prevent somewhat its heaviness in digestion.

GELATIN
Geletina

Gelatin is a highly refined food of a cold and dry nature, as we are told by the best authors, and hence highly suitable and useful for those with hot and moist temperaments, for young people and adolescents, and in the torrid season of southern regions. The blood that it produces is in some ways coldish, but it is particularly good for the secretion of bile which is the special property of gelatin. For this reason cooks should prepare it with skill and care, preferably from the flesh of pigeons. Take care, as it can cause colic and is harmful to the nerves, for which reason it should be served with a well-aged, aromatic wine.

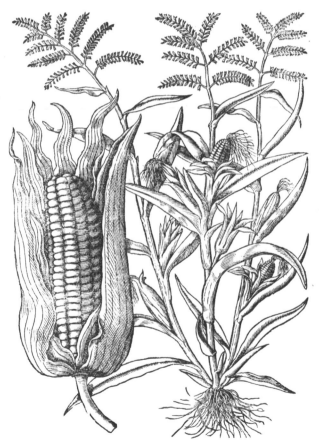

FRUMENTUM INDICUM

WHEAT
Frumentum

Nothing gladdens the heart of the farmer more than the sight of ripening grain under a cloudless sky. Wheat is life; an abundant crop means a bright future. Everyone, whatever their temperament or age, whatever the season or place, derives from wheat a food that is good for the blood, such as bread, *in primis*, or flour. The wheat must be ripe, grown in rich soil, free of any mixtures, its grains hard, heavy, full, smooth and shining, and of a golden color. Remember: *aperit apostemata emplastratum*, a wheat poultice will open up an abscess.

BARLEY
Ordium

RYE
Siligo

When it is the season for men and women to thresh the barley with the flail on the threshing floor, the grain will be good if it has been sown in rich soil (because it is the nature of barley to exhaust it), well ploughed, and dry. Then the barley will be very white, full, and heavy, which is the best kind, and easy to cook. The red variety is more resistant to the winter cold, but it is not as good. Barley is a food that produces *humorem bonum*, good humours, acts as a laxative, and is easily digested. It can cause some slight pain, but only if it has not been properly roasted before being ground.

The time for harvesting rye is difficult to establish, more so than for other cereals because as soon as the grains ripen they fall to the ground; moreover, the plants never ripen all at once. It is a food that generates thick humours which are *oppilantes*, or obstructive; it is suited to those with hot temperaments, and people who work, and yet it is beneficial because it suppresses the sharpness of the humours. Always choose newly harvested rye with large, firm grains, and to prevent it from being difficult to digest mix it with wheat. If the miller grinds it properly, it will make excellent bread.

CREAM OF BARLEY SOUP
Savich, id est pultes ordei

The flour that is made from barley is very beneficial to the flow of bile. Pliny spoke of it at length, saying that some people wash the barley first in water, leave it to dry overnight, then fry it, and, lastly, grind it; others wash the barley after it has been roasted and then grind it. It is important, however, to roast the barley in order to lessen its cold nature. Elsewhere we read that cream of barley soup, which is very suitable for sick people, should be made with twenty pounds of barley, three pounds of linseed, half a pound of coriander, salt as required, and the whole mixed well before grinding.

BARLEY WATER
Aqua ordey

Barley water is cleansing. Nutritious and easy to digest, it is given, with favorable results, to feverish patients to slake their thirst; it alleviates coughs and cleanses the lungs. It should be thoroughly boiled and light. Nevertheless, it easily turns sour and causes flatulence. To remedy this inconvenience, cook it together with hyssop and cinnamon; it is more nutritious if sugar is added. It benefits those with hot temperaments, especially in the summer and in southern regions because its nature, which comes from barley, is very cold.

53

ITALIAN MILLET
Panichum

This is one of the best-known cereals in Italy, and is almost exactly the same as millet except that the heads are tightly packed with racemes and full of vast numbers of little, round, hairy grains. There is a wild variety which is eaten only by the birds. The domestic kind is cold and dry by nature and not very nutritious. In the opinion of Galen, its benefits and disadvantages are the same as those of millet.

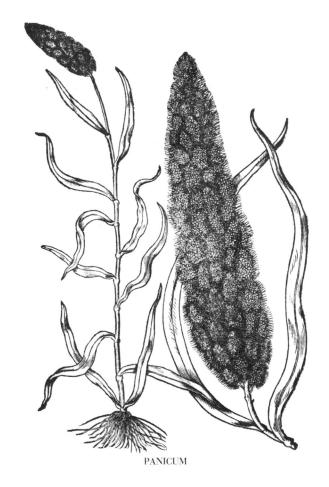

PANICUM

SORGHUM
Melita

The stalk is similar to a cane so that when a field of sorghum is ready for harvesting, it looks like a canebrake. The inside of the stalk has a white core similar to that of sugar cane. The head is full of seeds from which the peasants make flour and a very coarse bread that is difficult to digest and suitable for mountain dwellers who work very hard. A flat cake is made from the core, which has been reduced to a powder, with fresh pepper and eggs; eaten on the first day of the waning moon and for three or four moons, it is supposed to be a sure remedy for goiter.

MILLET
Milium

Owing to its nourishing qualities, millet thickens the blood, is good for the stomach, and quenches thirst, particularly if it is boiled in water. It is harmful to weak intestines and for this reason it should be well cooked and served with almond oil and sugar. Some believe it is less harmful if cooked with milk or with honey, or cooked in broth and served with good spices. But millet should be reserved for those with strong stomachs. Dioscorides mentions it only briefly, but manages to include this most useful cure: roast the millet and while still hot put it into a bag and apply to the body to relieve pain.

VETCHLING
Mesch, id est cicerchia

This is a food for the poor and hardly ever sampled by the rich. Nevertheless, vetchling gives relief to anyone with a cough and a fever, but is harmful *debilitati dentium*, to weak teeth. It is a nourishing food but weighs heavily on the stomach, causing vertigo. Soak overnight in water and cook with oil and garlic, mint or thyme, or dress with salt, pepper, mustard, and vinegar. It is suitable for strong stomachs and people accustomed to hard work. Those with delicate stomachs or leading a leisurely life should abstain from it.

CHICK-PEAS
Cicera

There are white, black, and red chick-peas. Large, full ones that have not been damaged or perforated by animals or insects are preferable. They heat the blood and promote strong sperm in the male (which is why the red ones are called venereous). The chick-pea *provocat urinam*, generates milk, and opens obstructions. *Facit ventositatem* and is harmful to ulcerations of the kidneys and bladder, which can be treated with celery, fennel, and, at other times, with poppy seeds. Soak the chick-peas in water overnight and cook with rosemary, sage, garlic, and parsley roots. Add boiled must and cinnamon to the broth, which is preferable to the chick-peas themselves.

LETTUCE
Lactuce

Lettuces differ in color; some have dark green leaves, others are whitish, and others have blood-red spots. If not transplanted on the fifth day after sowing, lettuce will not do well and is good only for the geese. It arrests the flow of bile, assuages thirst, and alleviates insomnia. It is better for the blood than any other vegetable. But it is harmful to the eyesight and sexual vigor; therefore, it is better to combine it with celery or fennel. According to Dioscorides, the lettuce seed takes away the venereous appetites that come in dreams. The ancient Romans, so Martial tells us, used *claudere coenas lactuca*, to finish the evening meal with lettuce.

LACTUCA FLORESCENS

LUPINES
Lupini

It is customary to sweeten lupines so that they may be eaten on any occasion, like confectionery. The best lupines are white and a good size; they thicken the blood, but this is considered more beneficial than the effects of eating lentils. Digestion is easy and passage through the intestines can sometimes be too rapid. The bitter flavor can be removed by adding salted water and vinegar. It is advisable to remember the advice of Dioscorides: that a drink of chopped and macerated lupines mixed with vinegar assuages stomach upsets and tempts the appetite. Wild or cultivated lupines are equally useful.

SWEDES
Napones

Swedes are a *satis bonum*, rather good, food suited to cold and dry constitutions of every age; there are two types: white and yellow. The white ones are larger and more attractive, but less tasty or pleasing to the palate than the yellow ones. The housewife will take care that the gardener gives her fresh ones from the garden. They are delicious cooked in broth made from fat meat and, although they bloat the stomach, they are effective in activating the bladder; if eaten with herbs and abundant pepper, they arouse young men to heights of sexual adventurousness. They can also be preserved with salt.

BEANS
Faxioli

As we know, there are different colored beans: white, red, yellow, and flecked with various colors. They are usually sown not only in the garden but other places as well, like loggias and balconies, because they are climbing plants that create agreeable shade and pergolas. Choose the reddish ones which should be free of insect holes, if they are for eating. They are fattening, cause nausea, heaviness of the head, and restless sleep. They make the blood sluggish, heavy, and bad. To lessen these undesirable effects season them with salted water, oil, and mustard, or with oil, vinegar, salt, and pepper.

PHASIOLI

FISH
Pisces recentes

Saltwater fish is superior to the freshwater variety and more nutritious. Nevertheless, always choose small, thin-skinned fish from waters with a rocky bottom. To prepare them, roasting over coals or a grill is better than boiling and boiling is better than frying, which is the least advisable way, especially for weak stomachs. When roasting fish, do not use a cover, but allow them to exhale their vapors. Never serve fish together with meat or milk or milk products or eggs. Fish is fattening, produces phlegm, and makes you thirsty.

PICKLED FISH
Pisces infusi in aceto

The nature of this food, which should be bought in town from fishmongers who prepare it with skill and honesty, can be said to be cold and dry, partaking of water and fire, if the fish have been roasted before being soused in vinegar; but they are cold and moist if they have been boiled. They must remain in the vinegar more than six days, because initially they hold a great deal of moisture which is part of their constitution. If roasted, they stimulate the appetite and are suitable for old people and those with cold temperaments, and, if boiled, are suitable for ardent young people.

SYRUP OF VINEGAR
Siropus acetosus

This should be prepared by a skilled druggist in a moderate decoction and appear clear and pure. It partakes of both the cold and hot, as is the nature of vinegar, and the more so by the use of fire in the preparation. It generates cold humours and at other times good ones, but mainly *subtiliat, incidit et mundificat*, it thins, reduces, and purifies bad humours; hence this syrup may be used by everyone regardless of age, and everywhere when opportune. The harm that it may cause—coughs, dysentery, and sexual impediments—can be remedied with juleps, that is, sugary syrups.

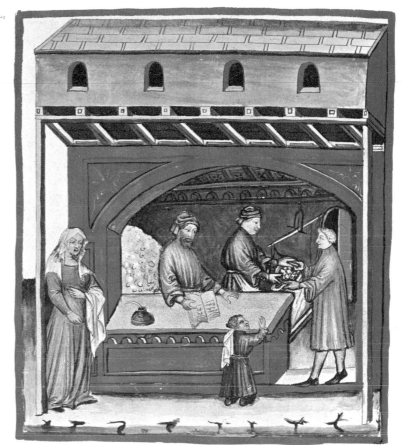

SALT
Sal

Salt is used daily to season all foods and also to preserve meat and fish and other things necessary to life. It may be sea or mineral salt or, though rare, from certain lakes or rivers. Dioscorides particularly valued salt from Cyprus, but today the salt produced from the banks of the Adriatic is thought to be better. It is hot and dry, partaking of fire, which extracts the moisture from it. It aids digestion and the passage of food, which it prevents from putrefying in the viscera. It causes *pruritum in cutis*, itching of the skin, and it can be harmful to the brain and eyesight.

VINEGAR
Acetum

Vinegar is cold by nature and therefore constricts and chills the body, but the very perceptive Galen maintains that it has opposing qualities, making it a mixed substance that incorporates the hot and cold, both delicate, but with the cold predominating. It should be made from strong wine and kept in barrels. It is useful in curbing excessive bile, it soothes the gums, and stimulates the appetite. Boiled, it produces vapors that are helpful for dropsy and relieve deafness and whistling in the ears; distilled, it kills worms; taken hot in the mouth, it cures toothache. It harms the nerves, which can be counteracted with water and sugar.

VERJUICE
Agrestium

This is made from sour grapes which have been harvested before the sun enters Leo. They are condensed by being left in tubs for several days together with the marc, covered with a heavy cloth, until the marc rises and the dregs are deposited on the bottom, clarifying the verjuice. It has constricting properties, especially when made from wild grapes. It is kept for a year and may be used either as a condiment or as a medicament. It generates *humorem modicum*, a moderate amount of humour, and is beneficial for an overly hot viscera, and yet it is harmful to the chest and nerves. These effects can be prevented if verjuice is accompanied by fatty or sweet foods.

WHITE WINE
Vinum album

Always choose white wine whose color verges on lemon-yellow. It heats the blood and assuages hunger; being light, it is useful for the stomach and easily distributes itself to all the body's members, as Dioscorides records. He also adds that of all the wines, white is deserving of praise, whether taken in good health or in sickness, and that it is always "a very salutary thing" to moisten food with a little wine. White wine is harmful only when taken in excess; but used properly, well tempered with water, it is beneficial at any time, for every age and every constitution, provided it has not been kept too long, in which case it is harmful to those with weak heads and members.

VITIS ALBA

63

SPRINGWATER
Aqua funtium

The housewives with their buckets should go to draw water from the fountains facing the east. As the ancient scholar and physician Hippocrates of Kos tells us, water has the qualities of cold and moisture in the highest degree, which it takes from the two elements of earth and air; thus it makes one cold and causes watery swellings which can be prevented *cum balneo*, with baths, and moderate exercise. It is good for an inflamed liver and the digestion and *multiplicat urinam*, it acts as a diuretic. "It is very useful and modest and precious and pure," as our good friars in their gray habits instruct us, and it is eminently suited to young people with a hot and dry humour, especially in the summer and in hot districts.

ROSE WATER
Aqua rosacea

At the right moment during the summer the women of the house will have prepared rose water, which is made from the most fragrant of the flowers in the rose garden and without adding water but using only their natural moisture. In this way the finest results are achieved. It provides relief in the summer heat because it does good to *virtutibus et ynstrumentibus sensuum*, the efficacy of the sensory mechanisms which, due to the high temperature, become sluggish; it comforts the heart, prevents fainting, and resolves it. Drinking rose water will irritate the respiratory passages, which can be soothed with a white julep (sugary syrup).

CAMPHOR
Camphora

STARCH
Amilum

Camphor is the gum that comes from the light, silky wood of trees in India, which are so large that an unimaginable number of people can find shade under them. At first it is stained with red, but then, with the heat of the sun or fire, it turns white. The best camphor is white, and has a penetrating smell. It helps to stop a nosebleed, inflammation of the liver, burning eyes, and high fevers. It causes insomnia, which can be remedied with a perfume of violets and water lilies. Keep tightly sealed or it will evaporate, which sometimes happens, to the chagrin of the careless chemist.

Starch is made, as Dioscorides instructs us, from three-month-old grain which has been carefully cleaned, washed five times in one day, and drained thoroughly. When the grain is soft, wash it and squeeze it out; wash it again and squeeze it out anew. The impurities that come to the surface are thereby removed and the starch is put to dry on some new tiles in the burning sun. It must then turn white and brittle. Starch has the properties of easing bilious attacks and, prepared with sweet almond oil, it soothes coughs. It produces a melancholic humour and unless sugar is added, it is heavy and slow to digest.

LINEN CLOTHES
Vestis linea

ROOMS FOR THE SUMMER
Camere estuales

A good house will have suitable rooms for the summertime where one can spend the morning hours. These rooms must be rather cold and nicely moist thanks to the convenience of a loggia or portico, or to the way they are built and protected from the sun by their orientation, by high ground, trees, or other buildings. The best rooms will have a temperature like spring. If one has rooms of this sort, they are beneficial to one's general well-being, and one's digestion in particular. If, however, too much time is spent in them, one loses the advantage that summer confers on the body: dissolving the humours.

Linen clothes are very suitable for the summer: they are light, splendid, and attractive. The women will see to the making of them, working rapidly and wisely with scissors and needle. Linen clothes are useful in keeping the body at a moderate temperature and they help to dry out ulcers, but they press on the skin and prevent the exhalation of vapors. For this reason it is wiser to make clothes from cloth that has a mixture of linen and silk, which also looks dazzlingly elegant.

66

FALL

And as the late leaves of November fall
      To earth, one after another, even fewer
      Till the bough sees its spoil gone past recall. . . .

Dante
Inferno, III, 117–119

Translation taken from *The Viking Portable Dante, The Divine Comedy*, translated by Laurence Binyon, Penguin Books, 1975.

When the sun enters the sign of Libra, at the beginning of the autumn, it is the time of the grape harvest. It is one of the distinct events marking the agricultural year, and it is accompanied by a tradition of fashioning allegorical images. In the calendar of twelve sculpted slabs, now in the Parma Baptistery, dating from two centuries before the Viennese *Tacuinum* and attributed to Benedetto Antelami, the man gathering bunches of grapes points to September, the first month in autumn. Another example from the Po Valley, the region of *The Book of the Cerruti Family*, depicts the same scene in one of the surviving reliefs from the "Door of the Months" from the Cathedral of Ferrara. The grapes are collected in a reed basket woven in the same manner as the basket which the woman with the apron around her waist offers, overflowing with grapes, to the grape treader in the illustration.

Of the four representations of the seasons, autumn is one of two that depict agricultural work, the other being summer: harvesting and grape picking, grain and vines, bread and wine. The remaining two show spring as an out-of-doors scene of trees and flowers, and winter as an indoor scene. The first depicts young people surrounded by nature, the second, an old man warming himself by the fire. The balancing of these allusions does not appear to be mere chance. According to the ancients' naturalistic philosophy of harmonies, to which we have already referred, seasons and elements form pairs in the following way: spring-air, summer-fire, autumn-earth, winter-water. One does not have to look too deeply into these pictures to find evidence of these relationships: for spring a bird flies through the air; for summer a young man with ears of corn in his hair like a halo looks like a symbol of the sun (the sun, generator of fire); for autumn, earth fills almost half of the picture and is also represented by the grape harvest which completes the agricultural cycle. In the winter scene there does not appear to be any reference to water, but this may not have been the case in the medieval mind. The bird that the family is holding by the neck is aquatic, perhaps a goose; according to the practice of *contraria contrariis*, we must reflect on the importance of the fire scene in which the old man warms his hands and the woman raises her skirts to warm her legs.

The etymology of autumn—*autumpnus* in the Viennese manuscript—recalls the presumed verb *autere*, meaning "to refresh" which, in the Indo-European languages, has an equivalent in Persian, and of which our word would be a passive participle. Ellbochasim maintains that autumn increases the melancholic humours, that is, the body's production of black bile: *melancholé* in Greek, which, of the four humours, corresponds to this season. Also it is harmful *dispositis ad ptysim*, to those predisposed to tuberculosis, who can prevent the effects *cum balneo*, among other things. These baths are therapeutic: "drawn with water," says Castor Durante da Gualdo, "they warm and moisten, relieve lassitude, resolve fullness, ease pains, mollify, fatten; they are suitable for young and old people before eating because they draw nourishment to the members and strengthen them."

GRAPES
Uve

The best grapes are white and full of juice and have thin skins. When possible, the vine is grown tied to a tree, but never plant cabbages in the vineyard because nature has interposed the cruelest hostility between these two plants. Grapes are good for the blood and very suitable for old people and, owing to their constitution, for people with cold temperaments. They cleanse the intestines and accelerate corpulence. The excessive thirst caused by grapes can be assuaged with sour pomegranates. Galen records that in the spring it is customary to eat the first shoots of the vine, which constitute an astringent food and are pleasing to the stomach.

THE FIG TREE
Fichus

The fig tree produces fruit without flowers on its farthermost branches after its leaves appear. Figs differ in shape and color, type of skin and pulp, but the best ones are white and should be washed and peeled before eating. Next in quality are the red ones, and lastly the black. They cleanse the kidneys of gravel, thin the humours, and protect against poison. They produce a feeling of fullness. Immediately after eating fresh figs, drink fresh water, which will temper their natural heat and cause them to descend to the bottom of the stomach; or eat pomegranates afterwards.

QUINCES
Citonia

The best quinces are large and full; they cheer the heart and stimulate the appetite. They also cause colic, which is remedied with dates sweetened with honey. Quinces, which are prepared in various ways, are not only suitable for the sick but useful and pleasing to the healthy. When preserving quinces over the winter, avoid putting them near grapes because their strong odor will contaminate the grapes and cause them to rot. It is said that pregnant women who eat plenty of quinces will give birth to industrious and highly intelligent children.

COTONEA MALUS

SWEET POMEGRANATES
Granata dulcia

There are two kinds of pomegranates: sweet and sour; the first is hot by nature, the second cold. Both types have a covering like red leather, and the inside is full of quadrangular-shaped grains that are red and winy. Of the sweet variety the large ones are preferable and easy to peel. They provide commendable nourishment and are useful for coughs. However, they cause swellings which can be counteracted with sour pomegranates. We find in some texts that whole pomegranates, put in the oven in a well-covered pot until they are burnt, make a very effective powder for treating dysentery. Take an eighth and a half of an ounce with red wine.

SOUR POMEGRANATES
Granata acetosa

Nature has established a very close friendship between the pomegranate and myrtle, which intermingle easily with each other, both becoming much more fertile. The very juicy sour pomegranates are preferable. They produce a moderate humour and are good for the liver. But they are harmful to the chest and this can be remedied with food sweetened with honey. They are a suitable food in very hot regions, especially for young people. Dioscorides relates that some people believe that three pomegranate flowers eaten while still very small will keep you from having diseases of the eyes for an entire year.

72

APPLES
Mala dulcia

We speak here of sweet apples, which are by nature moderately moist while sour apples, on the other hand, are cold and dry. Large and sweet-smelling and, above all, ripe apples are to be preferred. They stimulate the heart, but are harmful to the nerves. Apples that ripen in June are good for melancholic diseases and especially the syrup that is made from them is very cordial; those that ripen in the autumn and are cooked under the embers and mixed with a syrup of licorice, starch, and sugar are administered successfully for chest pains twice a day before meals. Apples are stored in straw, but must not touch each other or they will rot.

JUJUBES
Juiube

The jujube tree is only slightly smaller than the plum tree, and has thorny branches. Jujubes are similar to olives and, like them, have stones; they are green at first, then whitish and in the final stage yellow and finally reddish. Before they ripen the pulp is green and sharp-tasting, but when ripe, it is yellow and sweet. They have little nourishment, but are a favorite food of unruly children and are also very popular with women. The best ones are fairly plump and should be peeled. They generate phlegmatic blood and take away the blood's sharpness. They cause swelling which can be eliminated with raisins, the seeds having been removed, which are effective in this case, *propter subtilitatem*.

CHESTNUTS
Castanee

ACORNS
Glandes

Choose full, ripe ones which yield a food of average goodness suited to ardent temperaments, young people and children, to the winter and cold regions. Principally they stimulate the appetite, alleviate nausea and vomiting, are good for the chest and for *difficultati urine*. In fact because of their vapors, they can weigh heavily on the brain and stomach, but this can be avoided if they are roasted, stirring them over a lively fire of seasoned wood, and accompanied by a pinch of salt and a good, light wine.

Acorns from the oak tree are mainly food for pigs which develop solid, tasty meat. They are nonetheless of some immediate usefulness to man as well, though they are only of modest nutritive value. Choose fresh acorns that are large and full and eat them roasted and sprinkled with sugar. They are retentive. Dioscorides says of the acorn that a decoction prepared with the shells included and drunk with cow's milk is a good antidote for poisons; whereas chopped and made into a poultice, they soothe inflammations, and with hog's grease added they make a healing poultice for malignant ulcerations.

74

HAZELNUTS
Avelane

Not all hazelnuts taste the same; some are quite sweet and pleasant to eat, whereas others are bitter. They stimulate the brain and induce concupiscence. Eaten in excess, they cause dysentery, but chopped and taken with water and some dissolved honey, they help to soothe a cough; with pepper added they loosen catarrh. The oil from the hazelnut is very good for painful joints. It is written, but difficult to prove, that if a powder is made from the shells and it is incorporated with oil which is then applied to the forehead of children with gray eyes, their eyes will turn dark brown.

NUX AVELLANA

75

WALNUTS
Nuces

The ancient pagans called them Jove's acorns, perhaps valuing them because they came to eat them after true acorns in barbarous times. They are easier to digest than hazelnuts and more useful to the stomach, especially together with figs. They are good for a toothache and as an antidote to poisons, but they cause ulcers on the mouth, throat, and tongue. The remedy is white poppy seeds and sweet almonds. The oil obtained by crushing and squeezing out the walnuts is used for oil lamps and by carpenters for polishing; but heated and spread on swellings, it cures them.

NUTMEG
Nux indie

The tree is very similar to the peach tree and its fruit to the walnut, for it has a thick, green cortex, inside which is the nutmeg enclosed in a hard, thin shell. The fresh, sweet ones, says Ellbochasim of Baghdad, are preferable; they help the intellect and thin the blood considerably. The other authors agree that nutmeg sweetens the breath, is good for freckles, and fortifies the eyesight, the mouth of the stomach, the liver, and spleen. The liqueur that is made from crushed, heated, and pressed nutmegs gives off a delightful scent and is useful for coldness in the nerves, loosening the joints, and vigorously inflaming the male.

PINE NUTS
Pines

The domestic pine tree produces large, hard, pyramid-shaped cones which contain longish, white, sweet, and pleasant-tasting pine nuts enclosed within a strong shell. They are a good food that heats and thickens the blood; they are good for coughs and chest and lung inflammations and moisture. Pine nuts are also diuretic, maturative, calming, and laxative, as stated by Avicenna. They are harmful to the mouth of the stomach and blunt the appetite; to prevent this, combine the pine nuts with anise and raisins. It is an elegant custom of gentlemen to feed their caged birds with pine nuts.

BAY TREE BERRIES
Bacha lauri

The berries of the bay tree are similar to those of the olive tree: green at first and then black, but smaller and with a very large stone. The fully ripe, plump ones are more efficacious, having been grown in the sun. They are useful for cold stomachs and to relieve stomachaches, as well as pains in the intestines caused by cold or wind; they are also used to treat colic and, taken with honey, they are good for asthma and colds that arise from exposure to the cold and wet. According to the authors, seven berries of the bay tree taken by pregnant women who are near their time will ensure an easy delivery.

HORSERADISH
Rafani

Country people frequently eat horseradish with bread for it is one of nature's natural accompaniments to bread, like green oregano, watercress, garden thyme, wild thyme, pellitory, and rocket. In the winter it is served more as an accompaniment to foods and for the flavor it imparts to them than for nourishment. Wild horseradish is tougher and has a more pungent flavor than the garden variety which, freshly picked, is preferable. In fact it generates a bad humour. Its advantages are that, in appropriate circumstances, taken before meals, it causes vomiting; after a meal, it acts as a purgative, opens obstruction of the kidneys and removes the gravel, and stimulates the bladder.

RAPHANUS

78

CAPERS
Capari

The plump, as yet unopened capers that come to Venice from Alexandria in Egypt are reputed to be the best. Moreover, it is well-known that capers from very hot regions, like Arabia, are much more pungent than the Mediterranean ones and are more potent in heating the blood. They are usually pickled in brine, but are much more delicate when kept in very strong vinegar. They have the merit of strengthening the stomach and the appetite, opening occlusions of the liver, spleen, and kidneys, and killing worms. They are difficult to digest unless cooked with oil, vinegar, and herbs. Prepared in this manner, they are suitable for every age and climate.

ONIONS
Cepe

An excellent thing, the onion, and highly suitable for old people and those with cold temperaments, owing to its nature, which is hot in the highest degree, sometimes moist, and sometimes dry. The most desirable of the many varieties are the white ones, being rich in watery juices. They generate milk in nursing mothers and fertile semen in men. They improve the eyesight, are softening, and stimulate the bladder. Headaches, which are sometimes caused by onions, can be cured with vinegar and milk. Those suffering from coughs, asthma, and constrictions in the chest should eat boiled onions, or onions baked under the embers, served with sugar and a little fresh butter.

MOUNTAIN CELERY
Livistichum

It is an agreeable pursuit to roam the pleasant, wild countryside, picking plants here and there, stopping to talk here and there, especially if your companion knows about plants and their multiple properties. Should you find lovage or mountain celery—to be picked green, fresh, and fragrant—remember that because of its hot and dry nature, which places it between air and fire and between fire and earth, according to the philosophy of natural things, it heats the blood, *provocat urinam*, opens obstructions *epatis et splenis*, of the liver and spleen. The smell, however, *gravat caput*, makes the head feel heavy.

FENNEL
Feniculus

Pliny gives evidence of this: the health-giving qualities of fennel were discovered by observing snakes which, on eating it, threw off all signs of age and clouded vision and became sharp-sighted. But not only is it good for the eyes, purifying the eyesight, but it increases the milk of nursing mothers, acts as a diuretic for everyone, and *resoluit ventositatem*. Choose the domestic plant, fresh and flavorful verging on the pungent, and since it is digested slowly, take care to eat it *per bonam masticationem et contritionem*, chewing and grinding it up well. It generates bilious humours.

PARSNIPS
Pastinace

Parsnips are a very white, tasty root vegetable; certain varieties are red. They are grown in gardens for eating on abstinence days, as directed by the Church, when fish is not available. This is a curious habit, in that meatless days are supposed to be an opportunity to mortify the flesh, and the main property of parsnips, as the best authors tell us, is to excite in no small measure the fires of lust. The red, sweet ones are to be preferred and should be boiled for some time as they tend to slow down the digestion.

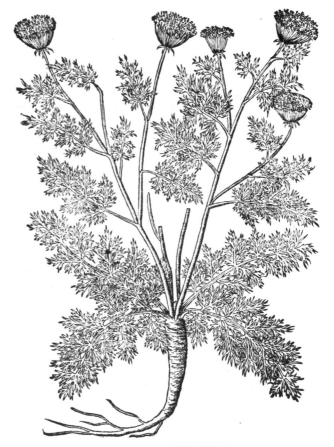

PASTINACA SYLVESTRIS

81

CAROB BEANS
Carube

The fruit of the carob tree, which German-speaking people call St. John's bread in the belief that it provided nourishment for John the Baptist in the desert, ripens in the autumn. When the beans are picked from the tree, many think the taste is abominable, but when they have been dried on the wickerwork shelves, they become sweet due to the liquid, similar to honey, that forms inside. They provide only mediocre nourishment and are suitable, it is said, for those who frequently ride horses. They are, however, difficult to digest and require some barley sugar. When fresh, they loosen the bowels, like cherries; when dry, they constrict them.

BANANAS
Musse

It is no surprise that Ellbochasim mentions this plant and its fruit, but as far as we are concerned we know of it only from texts or tales from merchants from Cyprus or pilgrims from the Holy Land. Sicilians, on the other hand, know them well. The leaves are fan-shaped and have a hard rib and a thin blade, which dries up in the summer. The banana has a yellow skin when ripe and white pulp. It seems at first to be very insipid-tasting, but then, they say that one can never eat enough of them due to their delicious flavor, which gradually emerges very pleasantly. They weigh heavily on the stomach, and their only virtue is that they are sexually arousing.

LICORICE
Liquiritia

We read in Theophrastus that the Scythians survived for ten to twelve days simply by chewing and sucking licorice, without any other food. We receive from Gargano the juice condensed into loaves and large bundles of the roots. But fresh licorice is the best, with roots that are neither too large nor too thin, tender and of uniform consistency. It is useful in treating hoarseness of the voice and throat; it is a diuretic; it cures constipation of the intestine and kidneys. It is good for the blood, but the juice causes nausea after a while and blunts the appetite. These disadvantages can be overcome by nibbling some raisins.

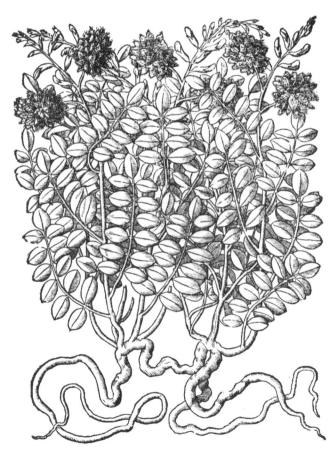

DULCIS RADIX, SIVE GLYCYRRHIZA

RICE
Rizon

Rice is *nutrimentum laudabile*, a praiseworthy fuel suited to every age and every land, but more so to people with hot, moist temperaments. Ask the grain merchant for the daisy white type that expands in cooking. Cooked in cow's milk or in sweet almond milk or in rich meat broth, it is more digestible and becomes more appetizing. It is very useful in cases of heartburn and dysentery, whereas it is harmful to anyone suffering from colic or constipation. A decoction of rice provides an excellent enema for acute intestinal pains.

TRUFFLES
Tartufule

Peasants tenaciously search for truffles not because they crave them particularly, but because rich men value them greatly and pay well for them. Pliny wonders whether truffles are not one of the earth's vices, a collecting together and condensation of itself, and he refers to the praetor Laertes Licinius who broke a tooth on a piece of money imbedded in a truffle. They go well with all foods and generate a heavy phlegm, which in any case the body burns quickly. Because of their earthy nature, they increase the melancholic humours, and this can be remedied by seasoning them with pepper, oil, and salt.

84

QUAILS
Qualee

PORK
Carnes porcine

Quail is eaten in the autumn, but do not overindulge. It should be young, plump, and well hung, pointed by hunting dogs or, better still, caught by birds of prey. Take care that it has not been raised on land where hellebore flourishes. Quail heats the blood and is very nutritious, putting weight on lean people. Some believe that it is suitable for the melancholic. Nevertheless, quail is troublesome to the stomach and must therefore be balanced with pomegranates, nuts, and cinnamon. Avoid quail in the summer when they are exhausted and feeding their young, for they can easily cause fevers.

When a pig is killed, the house has a wealth of different meats, hams, lard, and black pudding. Pork provides *copiosum* but moist nourishment. Choose gelded animals which have done a lot of running so that the muscle fiber is firm; avoid the suckling pig as its meat is excessively moist; meat from the sow is tough and full of melancholic humours. Pork is suitable for dry, thin physiques, but not for weak and phlegmatic stomachs, nor for anyone on a diet. Pork cooked over a grill with fennel and salt is a joyous and healthy dish.

85

DATES
Rutab, id est datilus

Ellbochasim, the scholar from Baghdad, discussed dates at great length, which is unusual but not surprising, yet the material only arouses our curiosity and is of little usefulness. In our part of the world the palm tree does not bear fruit because of the unfavorable climate. We are only familiar with the dates that arrive in Venice from Syria. Ellbochasim calls the ripe date *rutab*, which is beneficial to those with a cold stomach, suitable for cold and moist temperaments, very old people, the autumn and winter. It is harmful to the throat and voice, perhaps because of the moisture which is part of its nature together with heat. In this case one must prepare a decoction of poppy seeds.

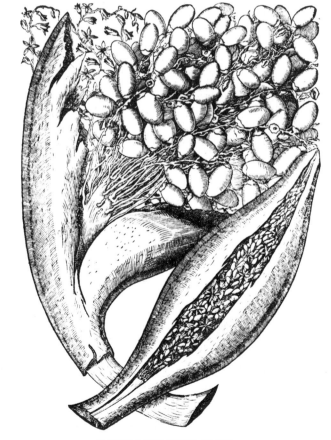

DACTYLI CUM PALMA ELATE

MORE ABOUT DATES
Cefalones, id est datili

Ellbochasim says this is the wild date. It should be sweet and fresh, and it stimulates the viscera, generating a thick humour. It is harmful to the chest and to remedy this, take another type of date and honeycomb. Concerning the *cefalones* we know from Theophrastus, illustrious teacher, pupil of Aristotle, and famous botanist, that there are other palm trees which not only bear a different sort of fruit but whose height and shape are different. There are palm trees with a tall trunk and lofty foliage and others with very short trunks but bearing more fruit.

ONE LAST WORD ABOUT DATES
Rusuri, id est datili

Dates that begin to turn sweet are called *rusuri* or *brusim* by Ellbochasim. Choose ones that are not astringent. They produce a moderate amount of blood, suit balanced constitutions of all ages, and they are beneficial in relaxing the intestine. Nevertheless, they are bad for the teeth and the mouth for which a syrup of vinegar is advised. As for their natures according to the philosophy of natural things, *rutab*, *cefalones*, and *rusuri* differ: the first is hot and moist, the second dry and cold or cold and moist, and the third hot and dry.

LAMPREY
Lamprete

The lamprey should be speared in waters that run over rocks; moreover, as some people say, it was called *lampetra* in the Latin of the classicists because of its habit of gliding over rocks. It is cold and moist, but less so than the eel. It generates a phlegmatic humour and is fattening and highly nutritious. It is excellent poached in Malmsey wine, its mouth shut with nutmeg, studded with cloves, and cooked in a frying pan with hazelnuts, bread, oil, spices, and more Malmsey.

THE SOUTH WIND
Ventus meridianus

The wind that blows from the south, and is also called "austral" by sailors, has a warm nature, partaking of the hot in the second degree, and is only moderately moist. It is suited therefore to cold and dry constitutions. It fleetingly comforts the infirm and is particularly agreeable when it blows in the autumn, interrupting the first drop in temperature. It is at its best when it has first passed *per bonan regionem* through regions of goodness: this must be carefully considered when deciding on where to spend one's holiday. It is good for the chest and agitates the senses, which can be comforted with camphor and rose water.

88

WINTER

The air weighed down and the unwelcome fog,
Compressed all round by raging winds,
Soon it is the moment that it turns to rain,
And already the rivers are become almost like crystal,
And instead of grassy valleys
There is naught to see but rime and ice.

Petrarch
Rhymes, sestina III, lines 1–6

In winter if the air is too cold, as sometimes happens, one avoids the wind, especially the north wind, and one does not go out before the sun has risen. The healthiest sites for a house are those facing south, and in any case one should reside on elevated land, not near the ground, or underground, or in dark places, but in areas filled with light and sun "because life is sustained in the open and in the light and man grows mouldy and wastes away in the darkness."

In the rooms strew herbs that suggest hotness, such as mint, pennyroyal, sage, hyssop, bay leaves, rosemary, marjoram. Make a decoction of these herbs, adding cloves, cinnamon, and nutmeg, with which to spray one's living quarters. A fire should always be lit with fragrant wood like laurel, rosemary, cypress, juniper, oak, pine, fir, larch, terebinth, and tamarisk. Such a fire will rectify the poor quality of air and thin or dissolve heavy, viscous humours of the body.

The nature of winter, when the season unfolds normally, is cold in the very highest degree, as well as moist. It is helpful for bilious illnesses and it encourages digestion, but it increases the flow of phlegm and is harmful for illnesses of the phlegmatic type. One protects oneself *cum igne et vestimentis*, with fire and clothing. The latter should be made of the skins of sheep, fox, or marten, but wool, cotton, and silk can also be used. Stockings should be made of rabbit skins which are very good for infirmities of the joints, or fox which is comforting for all the members. Gloves to cover the hands should also be made of fox skins. The body should be well covered during the day and night and especially the head, "which is the domicile of the rational soul from which most infirmities derive." Many suggest that the head should be kept twice as warm at night as during the day, and rightly so, because while we sleep the natural body heat withdraws to the interior parts, leaving the outer parts exposed to the harmful effects of the cold. Remember, too, that it is very harmful to expose your head to the moon's rays, especially when the moon is full on cloudless nights.

Perfumes are also important in winter; with their properties they open blocked pores, thin the humours, and are useful against cold and moisture. One should therefore burn incense over hot coals: cinnamon, laudanum, nutmeg, citron rind, myrrh, ambergris, aloe, musk. Or one can mix the above substances with resin from the trunk of a storax tree and place a little over the coals. Spray clothes with water distilled in wine with small quantities of zedoary, cinnamon, nutmeg, carnation, juniper berries, ambergris, and musk. Use a decoction of sage and rosemary in wine for washing the face.

Regarding food in the winter the concept *de mensa sume quantumvis tempore brume*, eat as much as you want in the winter time, holds true. In fact, in the winter when it is cold and damp, you need to eat a lot but drink little. And that little should be a robust wine.

ROOMS FOR THE WINTER
Camere hyemales

The rooms that one inhabits in the winter should be moderately warm. One must therefore see that the farmhands have ready in good time piles of well-seasoned and long-burning firewood; take care that it is quickly brought into the house, cut to the right size for the fireplaces. One could not ask for a better temperature for the rooms in winter than that of late spring, which reawakens the faculties numbed by the overly rigorous out-of-doors. Bear in mind that excessive heat in the winter produces an irksome thirst and causes food to be expelled from the body before it has been properly digested.

HOT WATER
Aqua calida

Hot water is very helpful and extremely comforting for reviving members that have become stiff with cold; it is especially pleasant as a footbath. But here we must remember the effects of hot water as a drink. It purifies the intestine, but generates moist swellings and *laxat instrumenta digestionis*, relaxes the digestive machinery. This disadvantage can be corrected by adding rose water, thanks to the astringent nature of the rose. The water should preferably be warm and fresh, originating from rainwater, as we have already said under that heading.

SILK CLOTHES
Vestis de sete

Silk clothing is very luxurious and grand. It is highly valued and equally highly priced and for this reason it cannot be worn by peasants, but only by noble men and women and esteemed and prominent citizens. *In medicina*, according to medical science, everything that was said about woolen clothes applies equally to silk ones, for the nature of silk, like that of wool, is hot and dry. Wool, however, is said to be better than silk for covering the head at night.

WOOLEN CLOTHES
Vestis lanea

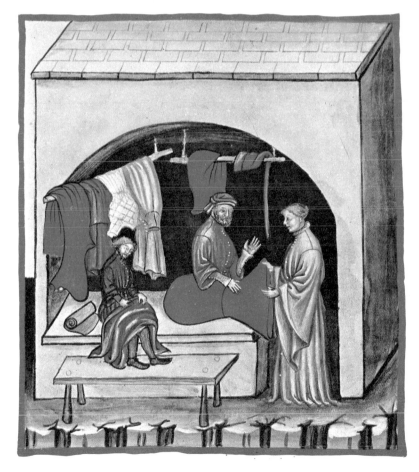

Clothes are suited to *praeparatio aeri*, or the adaptation of the climate to life, which is one of the seven things essential to good health. Clothes made of wool, whose nature is warm and dry, are beneficial in the winter to old people, life in northern regions, cold constitutions, all things that, of the four elements, correspond to water. These clothes, especially those in fine Flemish wool which are to be preferred, draw the inner heat from the body and keep it warm. The advantage of wool can also be a disadvantage: as too much warmth is harmful, wear a thin linen garment under the wool.

SNOW AND ICE
Nix et glacies

The nature of both these things is very cold and extremely moist; hence both are suited only to those with ardent temperaments and only in the summer and in southern regions. Snow and ice, being things of the winter and the north, very rarely have any use to which they can be put unless one has the costly opportunity of having them brought from their place of origin with all the ingenious devices required. They help to improve the digestion, if they originate from good, fresh water. They cause *vessicationem* to the joints and also paralysis; they also cause coughing, for which reasons one should take them only after drinking a moderate quanity of wine.

THE NORTH WIND
Ventus septentrionalis

The wind that blows from the north, greatly agitating the trees, is called the tramontane and is of a very cold and very dry nature. The best is a north wind that has first passed over expanses of fresh water before reaching the places where it is usually found: but that happens only where the lay of the land allows it. The north wind, unlike almost anything else, helps to clarify and sharpen the senses, and it is especially suited to young people. But it is harmful to the chest and brings on coughs. One can protect oneself with suitable clothing and also with baths.

GAZELLE
Carnes gazelarum

A gentle and mild animal which the Arabs consider, so we read, a paragon of feminine beauty, the gazelle is not to be found for hunting in our regions. Nevertheless, the authors tell us that its flesh is of a hot and dry nature and it is preferable if the animal is young. It generates strong blood; it provides various benefits in the winter because it wards off colic and paralysis and all of the illnesses that come from excessive moisture; lastly, it is effective against many excesses of the body. It is drying to the nerves unless one prepares it with oil and vinegary substances.

HARE
Carnes leporine

The hare should be caught young in the winter by dogs that exhaust it during the chase. The meat should be hung in the open at night. It is food that benefits *superatis a multa pinguedine*, those who are overcome by excess weight. Young hares are tender and easy to digest whether cooked in water and wine with sage, or roasted with sage and cloves, or in a pie. But hare tends to generate melancholic humours and is therefore not suitable for those temperaments. It causes insomnia which can be prevented if aromatic spices of a delicate sort are added in the right amounts.

ROAST MEATS
Carnes sufryxe

Roast meats are very nourishing and make the blood strong, but they are more difficult to digest than boiled meat and for this reason one should avoid eating large amounts. It is better to roast fatty meats and boil lean meat because fire consumes the fat of the former and water lends moisture to the latter. Roast meat is suitable for supper in that being arduous for the stomach it is better if it is digested, like any other food, at night. Roast meat, in any case, is suited to the winter and is good for constitutions and stomachs with a moist nature, by generating hot blood. The resulting thirst can be quenched with verjuice.

ROBUST RED WINE
Vinum rubeum grossum

Most gentle liquor, genuine sustainer of life, regenerator of the spirits, wine is more suitable for old people than for anyone else because it tempers the frigidity they have accumulated over the years. We cannot always agree with Galen, who advised wine to preserve the health of children and young people. In truth, it is like adding fuel to a fire. It should be mentioned that red wine ought to have a pale, transparent color. Specifically it helps to mitigate syncopes; it generates bilious red humours; it is harmful to those with weak livers and spleens, who can counteract the effect with sour pomegranates.

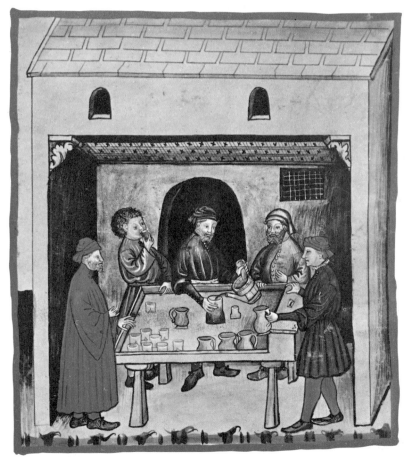

VITIS VINIFERA

OLD AROMATIC WINE
Vinum vetus odoriferum

When wine has been aged for more than four years, it gains in heat. That fragrant, powerful wine, which ought not to be bitter or vinegary but pleasing to all the senses, should be used primarily as medicine. When drinking it, always exercise moderation and dilute it with plenty of water. It thins and sharpens the blood; it cures pains in the eyes; *vivificat spiritus* revives the spirit; it is good for cold stomachs due to its hot nature. It is harmful to the senses and memory of children, but as we said previously about wine, it is better that the young and very young abstain. In each case the harm can be remedied with sour apples and lettuce hearts.

COW AND CAMEL MEAT
Carnes vachine et camelorum

Arab physicians discuss them together as they consider their natures to be exactly the same; that is, hot and dry in the second degree, but it is hard to believe that we would ever find camel meat at our butchers, who nevertheless provide very good cow meat. It is useful to learn about unfamiliar things. The best meat comes from young animals which have excercised a lot. It is suitable as nourishment for those who do tiring work and suffer from an excess of bile. It thickens the blood and makes it melancholic and therefore aggravates black bile illnesses. Sugar and pepper provide a remedy.

DRIED AND SALT MEAT
Carnes salite sicce

Meat that has been preserved by being salted down is by nature a degree drier than fresh meat. It is suited to the winter, to hot and moist temperaments, to young people, and northern regions where it keeps better. Make certain that fatty, moist meat is used when preparing salt meat. It is suited to phlegmatic temperaments who do tiring work. It produces melancholic blood and causes colic unless it is cooked with oil and milk, or in broth into which butter and eggs have been mixed. Lastly, never cook salt meat with lentils: this combination causes horrendous and fearful dreams.

CALF'S HEAD
Capita

BRAINS
Cerebra animalium

This is one of those foods whose individual parts display different natures, and are consequently slow and difficult to digest. Whether it is a calf's or sheep's, billy goat's or kid's head, this is the case. For this reason it generates a combination of humours depending on the constitution of each part. Even light foods eaten at the same time become indigestible; it causes belching. It must therefore be seasoned with cinnamon, pepper, and aromatic substances and, after eating it, one should chew mastic. However, it has its benefits for it stimulates the action of the belly and purges it.

Whatever the animal, the brain of a fully grown specimen is to be preferred. This food produces phlegmatic, viscous blood, but it is useful because it is fattening and increases the cerebral matter. It can be harmful because it is difficult to digest, it easily produces nausea, and it rapidly spoils. Therefore, season it with salt, oregano, wild penny-royal, and spices of a hot and subtle nature. The brains of small birds, especially if they are mountain birds, are considered very good prepared as above and with vinegar, which takes away the moisture.

EYES
Oculi animalium

Few people eat eyes, except for those of the kid. In fact, they make the blood sluggish and cause nausea, but they can be beneficial because they increase the male seed. *Mediocriter eminentes*, the moderately bulging ones are preferable and their disadvantages are counteracted with oregano and salt or a sauce in which pepper and thyme, salt and vinegar are combined. While we are talking about the qualities of the animals' different parts, it is appropriate to recall a thought of Rufus: "Regarding the limbs of animals, the most laudable are those of the males and especially their middle parts and the tongues which offer good, moderate nourishment."

HEART
Corda animalium

It has a fibrous, tough substance and therefore the heart of an unweaned animal is preferable. It is very suitable for robust young people, during cold winters, and for people who work hard, because once digested, the body derives considerable nourishment from it. To prevent any harmful effects to the stomach and digestive viscera, the housewife, having purchased some from the butcher, should prepare it with vinegar, oregano, and hyssop.

TESTICLES
Testiculi

The essential nature of testicles is similar to that of the udder and they provide excellent nourishment, plus the fact that they strengthen the male seed and arouse sexual desire. It is said of rooster's testicles, which have a mild flavor, that *tantum nutriunt, quantum ponderant*, every ounce is valuable nourishment. The testicles of old animals are difficult to digest. They should be cooked first with wild pennyroyal and salt and then fried with fresh butter, or stewed with a vinegar sauce. Very old people and those with phlegmatic temperaments should not eat them.

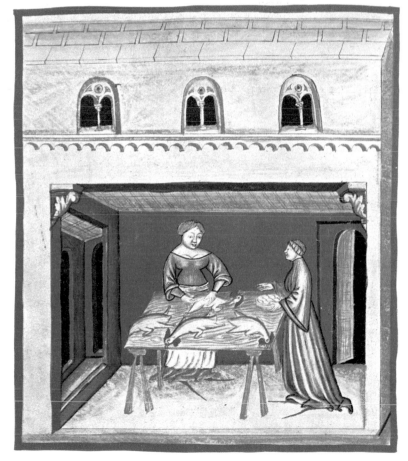

UDDER
Ubera

Many people are very fond of this dish, especially sow's or cow's udder, when it has milk, but it must be a young animal. It lies heavily on the stomach and is difficult to digest, moving slowly through the body; therefore, always prepare it with oregano and vinegar. It is, nevertheless, a nourishing food. It is a very good dish for women who require milk for their babies, provided their digestion can bear it.

101

CABBAGES
Caules onati

Some people think that cabbage is very useful against any sort of illness. Among these is certainly Chrysippus, the skillful Roman physician who wrote an entire book on the cabbage. Ellbochasim records only that cabbages are bad for the blood and their only virtue is that *aperiunt opilationes*, they open obstructions. In Dioscorides we read that if cabbage leaves are chewed and the juice swallowed, this will restore a lost voice; elsewhere we read that cabbage juice cooked with honey and used very sparingly as eyedrops clears the eyesight. The grape vine hates cabbage. Theophrastus, Varro, and Pliny all say that if you plant the vine nearby, it will move away.

BEETROOT
Blete

There are white, black, and red varieties. The red ones are much appreciated when thinly sliced in salad, being first boiled in water or cooked under hot embers, thinly sliced, and dressed with oil, vinegar, and salt. The white sweet ones are the best. Their juice *aufert furfures capiti*, removes dandruff from the scalp and loosens the belly. With regard to this last point, some recommend that the root be scraped with a knife, and covered with honey and a little salt, to be used as a suppository. The disadvantage of beetroot is that it hinders digestion, because of its moisture and laxative nature, and it heats the blood. It is suited to the winter and to old people.

SPINACH
Spinachie

The usual way to cook spinach is in a pan without any water, especially when it is tender. Spinach is so full of juice, which is drawn out by the heat, that it cooks in its own liquid. Garden spinach is best when *infuse in pluvia*, bedewed with rain. It is fairly nourishing and good for coughs and the chest. It is true that it spoils the digestion and if you normally suffer from this sort of thing, the spinach should be fried with salted water, or with vinegar and spices. The water from the spinach is useful against spider and scorpion bites when drunk, and is also helpful if sprinkled directly on the bites.

SPINACIA

SPLEEN
Splenes

LIVER
Epata animalium

It is pleasant to eat because it has a special tart flavor of its own, but it generates a bad and melancholic humour. It is suited to people with moist and fiery temperaments *ad ingrossandum complexionem et humores*, for fortifying the constitution and humours. It should not be used too much in foods that are melancholic because it is a depository for this type of fluid. Always choose the spleen from young, fat animals, especially the pig which is the least harmful, and cook it with fat and a lot of oil.

Goose liver from geese fattened with milk and pasta is excellent. Then, in order of goodness, come chicken liver and pig liver, from pigs fed on figs. Lastly, goat liver is most useful to *non videntibus de nocte*, those who do not see well at night. For this problem Dioscorides advises bathing the eyes in the juices that flow when roasting goat liver. He values asses' liver roasted and eaten on an empty stomach as a remedy for epilepsy. Galen maintains that wolf liver, dried and taken in powdered form, is "a divine thing" for hepatic fluxes and dropsy. Liver always purifies the blood.

TRIPE

Intestina id est busecha

The best tripe comes from a fat animal that has fed on good pastures and been butchered in its prime; the tripe should be thoroughly cleaned and cooked a long time in a rich broth with mint and abundant herbs. Kid provides the best tripe, then calf, and lastly cow. Tripe generates thick phlegm and is useful for those who have a fiery stomach *in quo cibus fervet*, in which food heats up. Tripe is a cold-weather food, especially for those who do hard physical work, but it is harmful for anyone with varicose veins, that is to say, *grossas venas involutas in cruribus*, or large knotted veins in the legs.

FAT AND LARD

Adeps et pinguedo

Generally fat and lard, which should come from select and well-nourished animals, are moist and hot in the human body to a greater or lesser intensity, depending on the nature of the animal from which they come. Pork fat and lard are more suitable for young boys, women, and anyone else who has soft flesh; by contrast, beef fat suits laborers, hoers, harvesters, and all those whose flesh is hard constitutionally or because rough living has conditioned it. Nevertheless, fat and lard are converted to smoke, and eaten on their own, cause obstructions. As nourishment it is excellent.

CREAM OF WHEAT SOUP
Savich, id est pultes tritici

Soup made from wheat is a winter dish, especially for old people and generally for those with moderate constitutions. Wheat, by its nature, provides solid nourishment that is outstandingly fortifying. It is good for those with moist intestines and should be prepared over a lively fire, with frequent stirring, using wheat that has been moderately toasted. It irritates the chest, and this may seem to contradict what other authors have written about wheat flour which, cooked in milk, soothes throat irritations and coughs, and helps to cure chest ulcers and spitting up of blood.

TAGLIATELLE (NOODLES)
Trij

The housewife kneads the dough on a table with vigorous movements, and from time to time the young girls turn the noodles with light fingers as they hang them on the racks to dry. The dough—*trij* in Arabic—is rich in nourishment and suited to those with hot stomachs, young people, the winter, and all regions. It is good for the chest and throat and is harmful only to people with weak stomachs or weak intestines, in which case barley sugar is the remedy. This is a food that should be *complete operato*, thoroughly and carefully prepared.

SPELT
Spelta

It looks almost exactly like wheat, except that its stalk is thinner and at the same time stiffer. Galen refers to it, explaining that its merits lie between those of wheat and barley. It is good for the blood and one should choose the large-grained, heavy, ripe variety. It is less nutritious than wheat, but it is beneficial for the chest, lungs, and those suffering from cough. It may be harmful to people with weak stomachs, but this can be prevented by eating it with anise.

BOILED WHEAT
Frumentum elixum

The great value of wheat to human life is apparent not only from people's experience of it but from reliable authors who also point out the merits of wheat from different regions. Pliny favors Italian wheat over all others for its whiteness and weight. And it is therefore very suitable for the preparation in question: boiled wheat. It should be *complete cocto*, well cooked, and it will give substantial nourishment, highly useful for tired bodies. It produces milk in nursing mothers and strong sperm in men.

CELERY
Apium

Pliny writes of the approval celery has always had when its "stalks are swimming in broth." It is very pleasing in condiments; by itself, it provides only modest nourishment which, nevertheless, because of its hot and dry nature, is suited to the winter, no less than to old people and to those with cold temperaments. Choose *ortolanum*, celery you have carefully grown in the garden and which is also attractive to look at. Its principal benefit is that it opens the body's obstructions. Serve celery with lettuce to prevent it from causing headaches. The pagans offered it up as food for the dead.

LEEKS
Pori

Choose pungent-smelling leeks from the mountains. They act as a diuretic and an aphrodisiac. Cooked and mixed with honey and swallowed slowly, they help to cure chest problems and get rid of catarrh by cleansing the passages of the lungs. Cooked under the embers, they can, as some believe, overcome the poisonous effects of fungi and act as a remedy for overeating and excessive drinking. But the brain and one's senses may suffer; therefore sesame or sweet almond oil should be provided. Leeks heat the blood.

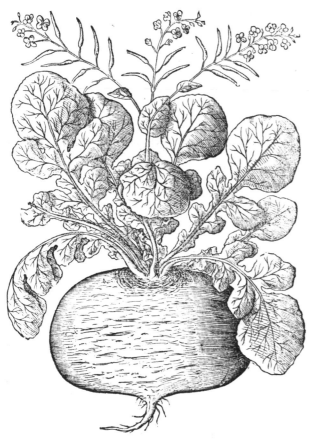

RAPUM ROTUNDUM

TURNIP
Rape

Like the leek, the nature of the turnip partakes of the hot, but to a much more modified degree, and whereas leeks are dry, the turnip is moist, sometimes to a very high degree. Turnips can be kept for a whole year if they are prepared in vinegar or brine. The best are sweet-tasting and thin-skinned. They are beneficial to the stomach and to dry intestines and *provocant urinam*, as a diuretic. They need to be cooked a long time or, better still, twice; if not properly cooked, they are difficult to digest and cause flatulence and swelling. If these problems are encountered, take an emetic or vinegar and salt.

MILLET BREAD
Panis milj

In the town of Verona, the bakers make a bread from millet flour which, eaten hot directly from the oven, leaves a sweet taste in the mouth. It has to be prepared skillfully with flour made from fine, fresh, pearly grains. It nourishes the intestine and is astringent. It descends from the stomach with difficulty; therefore one must, in the event, take physical exercise, baths, and eat it *rebus unctuosis*, with oily substances. Woodcutters and coalmen who work at the iron furnaces in the Non Valley will swear that there is no other food like millet bread with milk to give them sustenance for their labors.

UNLEAVENED BREAD
Panis azimus

When the children of Israel took leave of Rameses, they baked "unleavened cakes of the dough which they had brought out of Egypt for it was not leavened, because they were thrust out of Egypt and could not tarry" (Exodus, XII, 39). Unleavened bread has to be salted and well cooked. It restores tired bodies after hard physical labor. It is good for those with hot temperaments, young people who are growing, people who do heavy work, like cutting wood, and everyone in the winter and in cold countries. It may produce a bloated feeling in the stomach, and constipation. The remedy can be found *cum vino veteri bono*, in good, well-aged wine.

MATURED CHEESE
Caseus vetus

There is a saying: *Caseus est sanus, quem dat avara manus*, cheese is good for you provided you eat it in moderation. This applies even more to matured cheese, which should be tasty, provide hearty and substantial nourishment, and is more suited to young working people than to old retired people. It is painful to the kidneys, and causes obstructions and calculi. It is, nonetheless, less harmful if served with walnuts, almonds, apples, and pears. If eaten between meals it will not cause any inconvenience; however, *si secunda die comedatur raffanus, removetur nocumentum inductum per caseum*, eating horseradish the day after will remove any harm caused by the cheese.

BUTTER
Butirum

Butter from sheep's milk is highly prized and good for you because it rids the lungs of superfluities produced by colds or dryness of the air; it cures coughs and chest irritations, particularly if eaten with honey and bitter almonds. But *ebetat stomachum*, it stuns the stomach, reduces its function, and takes away the appetite. Too much butter brings on nausea and predisposes one to scabies and leprosy. Butter can be preserved by cooking it with salt; prepared in this fashion, it will retain its power to open and cleanse the chest.

111

ALMOND OIL
Oleum amigdolarum

The druggist, as Dioscorides tells us, will prepare the oil from clean, dry almonds, which he pounds in a mortar with a wooden pestle. He will add warm water, allow it to rest, and pound again. At this point the almonds are squeezed out in a small press, and then more water is added, and they are squeezed out again. Unfortunately, not everyone uses this fine old method. They do not clean the almonds properly or they heat them in a copper vessel over a fire that nearly chars them, without realizing that by trying to save time, they are perverting all of the qualities of the oil which generates temperate humours and is good for the stomach, chest, and coughs. It is harmful to those with weak intestines.

OLIVE OIL
Oleum olive

If made from ripe olives, its nature is hot and moist, but made from unripe olives, it is cold and dry. The former should be clear, fragrant, and tasty; it softens the stomach and kills worms. It rapidly turns into bile, takes away the appetite, and weakens the stomach. When aged, its level of heat increases, and it is more suitable as medicine than as food. Olive oil from unripe fruit, which is called *onfantinum*, should be pale and clear with a good smell, but a little sour-tasting. It is useful as a food for healthy people, it soothes the stomach and the gums, and makes a good chyme; and as a liniment, it stops perspiration. It obstructs the spleen and kidneys, for which cinnamon should be provided.

BLACK OLIVES
Olive nigre

Olives, like olive oil, have a dfferent nature, depending on whether they are ripe or green. The former are suited to old age, the latter to youth; both are suited to the winter and cold regions and the latter to hot places as well. The best olives are grown in a temperate climate. Ripe olives stimulate the appetite, but cause headaches and tend to cause insomnia. These disadvantages can be avoided by eating them with or before other foods. Green olives should always be eaten *praecedant alia cibaria* with other foods, otherwise they are difficult to digest. Seasoned, they stimulate the appetite.

OLEA SATIVA

113

CHICKEN EGGS
Ova galinacea

The white and yolk of an egg have slightly different natures: the yolk is nourishing, easy to digest, and pleasant-tasting, whereas the white is of difficult digestion. Hens' eggs are preferable to all other eggs; they are a rapid restorative, they are comforting, they increase the male sperm, and reinvigorate the sexual act. An excellent way to cook them in their shells is to boil them until just set, as hard-boiled eggs cause obstructions. The best way to cook them without their shells is to break them into boiling water; fried in butter or oil, they cause belching.

GOOSE EGGS
Ova anserum

After chicken eggs, the best are partridge and pheasant followed by duck, goose, and other aquatic birds' eggs, which are also very nourishing if one manages to digest them. Dove eggs are used more for medical purposes than as food; peacock and ostrich eggs have a very nasty taste. To return to goose eggs, they are suitable in the winter, for young people, and they increase the production of blood. They should be eaten *semiassa*, partially fried, and are helpful to those who work or exercise a great deal. Season them with oregano and salt to avoid *colice*, colic, gas, and dizziness.

DUCKS AND GEESE ❧
Anates et anseres

The young ones that have not yet left the nest are the most delectable. They are rich in nourishment of the phlegmatic kind and will put weight on those who are too thin. They fill the body with superfluities, to avoid which one blows borax into their beaks before killing them and then roasts them, filling the cavity with many herbs and spices (to dissolve the aforementioned superfluities), such as cloves, sugar, cinnamon, juniper berries, rosemary, marjoram, hyssop, and other similar ones. The liver of the duck is a delicacy, the breast and brains excellent; the liver and webbed feet of the goose are excellent cooked with yellow-rattle.

ROOSTERS
Galli

The best are the young roosters that crow with moderation. The old ones, if boiled with salt, wild saffron seeds, and cabbage, are good for people who suffer from colic. They are, however, harmful to the stomach unless you make them tire themselves out by scratching about before being butchered. Young roosters starting to crow and hens before they begin to lay provide excellent nourishment, which is very convenient in the winter, especially to the old. Of the egg-laying chickens, those that have been fed on good grain are always to be preferred. They increase the male sperm, fortify the brain, and are good for the blood.

RAISINS
Passule

There are different kinds, like sweet Damascene, Candia, and Cyprus raisins. Some people maintain that the plump raisins from Gerasa are the best. But one should know that not all raisins have the same qualities, the sweet variety being one kind and the harsh another; and they may also be with or without seeds. Furthermore, as Galen tells us, the nourishment that we get from raisins has the same property as their nature: sweet and more abundant from the sweet; harsh and less abundant from the harsh. Raisins heat the blood, help to soothe pains in the intestines, and fortify the liver and stomach. They tend to burn the blood, which can be corrected with fresh lemons.

DRIED FIGS
Ficus sice

Dried figs are suited to the winter. In September they are left to dry in the sun on rush matting. Some dried figs are imported by sea. Some people set great store by the round kind from Tartary, others favor the large white ones. They heat the blood moderately and sometimes to a high degree. They are good for the chest and offer protection against poison. They are harmful when they cause constipation, flatulence, and scabies. Walnuts and almonds are a good remedy for these things. It is well known that two or three dried figs left to soak overnight in aquavit and eaten the next morning are a wonderful aid for asthmatics.

LEMONS
Citra

Lemons are very similar to citrons in their shape and qualities, but they are smaller, juicier, more sour-tasting, and their peel less fleshy. The best quality is very fragrant and has a fine lemon-yellow color. They provide limited nourishment, but improve the flow of bile. A syrup is made from the juice, which is useful for contagious and pestilential fevers. A water is distilled from lemons which cures scabies and which women use, with much success, to improve their appearance. Juice squeezed from bitter lemons and drunk with Malmsey wine is effective in expelling kidney stones.

LIMONIA MALA

PIGEONS
Puli columbini

When possible select pigeons from dovecotes or use semi-domesti-
cated ones, *acquirentes iam sibi cibum*, when they have left the nest
to feed themselves. Their hot nature makes them useful against the
paralysis that comes from the cold. They heat the blood or, rather,
they inflame it and are therefore harmful to the brain and cause
restless insomnia, especially if roasted. They are far less harmful
if the heads are removed before cooking, or if cooked in rich stock,
or stewed with verjuice, plums, and black cherries, or with vinegar
and coriander. For some people, wild pigeons are good for weak
eyesight.

SMALL BIRDS AND THRUSHES
Avicule et durdi

When winter comes, choose thrushes that have grown fat on juniper berries and myrtle. Regarding small birds, we know generally
that the mountain ones, which are hotter and drier, are better than
those from the plains, ponds, or swamps, whose flesh is full of superfluities. The mountain variety thins the blood, is easy to digest,
and provides substantial nourishment, which is very suitable for
convalescents. Both should be roasted with sage and bacon. Their
effect is to strengthen men's libido and their reproductive possibil-
ities, though they are harmful because of malignant moistures.

PEACOCKS
Pavones

The peacock is valued as an ornament for the parks of rich men because of the male's beautifully colored tail rather than for any useful purpose. In fact, they cause damage to gardens and orchards and their meat is the most difficult to digest of all fowl. Despite this, they are very nourishing, especially for young people with a hot stomach, who are always measuring their strength in sports. Choose young peacocks that have been raised where the air is good and that have been hung in the same manner as the crane: by the neck with a stone attached to the feet, for a few days in the wintry air. Roast them with cloves and other spices.

THE CRANE
Gru

With regard to birds, always avoid the mating season, as birds exhaust themselves and do not eat and thus cannot provide substantial nourishment. They are, however, very suitable for the winter, their nature being hot. Such is the crane, which is good for people who work hard and exercise. As it is difficult to digest, it has to be hung overnight by the neck with a stone tied to its feet and then cooked with abundant aromatic herbs. It should be caught, using the falconer's art, with a bird of prey, although it is often brought down in the fields with a bolt from a crossbow.

119

TURTLEDOVES
Turtures

To trap the turtledove, it is customary to arrange the nets in a clearing with birdseed on the ground as a lure. The hunter, quiet and alert, remains hidden in some bushes, ready to pull the ropes to close the trap. For eating purposes, he will take the young ones that have just begun to fly. They are highly nutritious, though not as much as doves; fried rather than roasted, they are good for nervous illnesses; with wax as a stuffing, they are helpful in curing dysentery. Old turtledoves are harmful to those with melancholic temperaments because of their overly dry meat.

BITTER ORANGES
Cetrona

Their nature is cold and moist, in contrast to citrons which are also called "Median apples," that is, apples from Media, but have a cold and dry nature. Bitter oranges generate cold humours, are helpful for bilious stomachs, and harmful to phlegmatic ones. They are best suited to young people and to those with hot and dry temperaments, as anyone acquainted with medicine and its strict principles will understand. They are to be preferred ripe, as is always the case with fruit.

MEDICA MALUS

CITRONS

Nabach, id est cedrum

Large and aromatic, citrons improve the flow of bile but slow up the digestion, which can be prevented with the use of honeycomb. They produce melancholic humours. Pliny observed that in his time there were no citrons growing in Italy, despite diligent efforts to transport the plants from Media. The ancients were convinced that citrons were highly efficacious as an antidote to poisons. There is an account in the texts of two Egyptian criminals who were sentenced to die and the sentence was to be carried out in the usual way, with the bite of an asp. One escaped death, thanks to his having eaten a citron. From this incident, people learned about the power of the citron.

SALT FISH

Pisces saliti

It is customary to preserve certain fish by packing them tightly in barrels with a plentiful amount of salt; this dries the fish and keeps them from rotting. They are not, of course, very nourishing, but those left for a long time are preferable. They are good for people with phlegmatic temperaments because they liquefy and dry out the excess phlegm. However, they produce humours that cause dark spots on the skin, and are harmful because they cause impetigo and scabies. Boiled red wine is believed to be a remedy. The nature of salt fish is hot and dry, and therefore suitable for constitutions dominated by the cold and moist, as well as for old people and in winter.

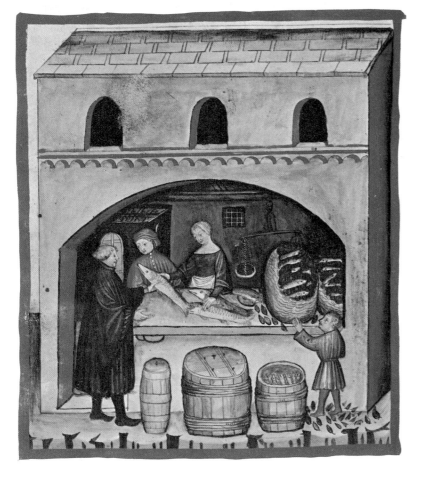

SALT WATER

Aqua salsa

Ellbochasim says that salt water is best when free-flowing and not bitter. It washes out the stomach and dries it. It makes one thirsty and causes obstructions; it causes itching and hurts the eyes, and should therefore be mixed with good clay and followed by a bath. Dioscorides reasons differently about seawater, which he says is beneficial as a bath for those whose bodies are swollen from a long illness; that warm salt water activates a sluggish intestine; that hot salt water will ease pains in the body. Some find it purges the body when heated, mixed with vinegar, wine, or honey, and administered immediately after chicken or fish broth.

AMBERGRIS
Ambra

Ambergris at its best is gray, light, and oily. It makes one bold; it revives weakened members and, equally, the nerves; its smell invigorates the heart and brain; it increases the intellect and helps melancholics. There are different opinions about its origins: one, that it grows on the bottom of the sea rather like mushrooms on land, and the movement of the waves pulls it out of the depths and deposits it on the shore; another opinion agrees with these origins, but says that shrewd fishermen extract it from the stomach of a fish which dies immediately after eating it; a third opinion states that it originates from certain springs.

CANDLES
Candele

Wax candles are of a hotter substance than tallow ones; *non tamen debent graduari in complexione, inquantum sunt candele*, it is an idle point, dealing with candles which are man-made, to classify them by degrees, as this applies only to natural objects. Tallow candles give a better and clearer light, which is less harmful to the eyes. They banish the darkness and one can then pursue nocturnal work. They weaken the eyesight, which can be rested by looking at dark green. They embolden the heart because they overcome the dark and the fears that it inspires.

THERIACA
Triacha

Galen praised this opiate medicament above all other antidotes, saying that it lived up to "everything it promises; nor did anyone who had been bitten by a wild beast, which usually kills men, ever die having then taken theriaca, nor did anyone ever die who first took it and was then bitten shortly afterwards." Apart from poison, it is effective against pestilential fevers, paralyses, and melancholy. When aged for more than ten years, which is the best kind, it causes insomnia, which can be remedied *cum infrigidantibus*, with potions that generate cold, like barley water.

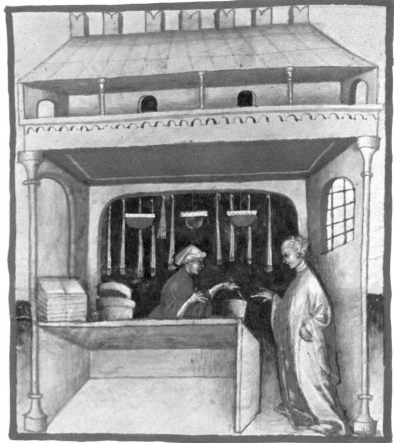

MUSK
Muscus

The very useful musk may be obtained from the druggist, but it comes from the distant lands of the East, as *est muscus apostematis gazelle cum maturus est*, it is the glandular secretion that comes to maturation in a certain species of gazelle. It is collected from the rocks against which the animal rubs himself to relieve the itching on the spot where this singular gland occurs. The musk is perfect at that moment, wth a darkish red color and a strong smell. It invigorates the heart and the brain and increases the faculties.

124

AND FOR ALL THE SEASONS

Comfort abounding in my heart,
    Joy and Delight
    In soule and spright
I did possesse in every part;
O Soveraigne Love by thee.
    Thy Sacred fires,
    Fed my desires.
    And still aspires
Thy happy thrall to bee.
    Love, I found such felicity. . . .

Boccaccio
The Decameron, Day Eight, lines 4–9,
    Conclusion.

Translation taken from *The Decameron*, Preserved to Posterity by Giovanni Boccaccio, Translated into English Anno 1620, Published by David Nutt, 1909.

The art of illumination is entitled *gaudia*, or joy. In *The Book of the Cerruti Family*, along with the plants, grains, fruits, herbs, meat and its divisions, fish, wine and water, habitations and clothes, winds and seasons, which we have looked at so far, there is another small group of images which penetrates even deeper into the customs and ways of thinking of those distant times and at the same time attempts to complete, with encyclopedic ambition, the universe of things on which our health depends. It is worth recalling that of the six things essential to life mentioned in the introduction to this book, the third says *rectificatio motus et quietis*, the right balance between activity and rest, the fourth *prohybitio corporis a sompno et vigiliis multis*, avoidance of overly long periods of sleep and wakefulness, and the sixth, *regulatio persone in moderatione gaudii, ire, timoris e angustie*, moderation in expressions of joy and anger, fear and anguish.

The treatment of this subject matter is brief, almost as though Ellbochasim, who was a theologian as well as a physician, nevertheless felt less confident in areas bordering on ethics, psychology, and personal freedoms than in areas where material things—food, drink, qualities, and effects—offer more empirical comparisons. These themes, seen as a whole, provide a singular picture. The only feelings treated are joy, wrath, and shyness, of which the first two are spontaneous and natural and the third is cultural; then activity, wakefulness, and sleep, the last accompanied by talking in one's sleep and evening conversations that prepare one for sleep; followed by two reactions of bodily distress, drunkenness and vomiting, and a handful of "amusements" or pastimes such as contests, horse riding, hunting, listening to and making music, singing, dancing (for this last item the effects of watching rather than participating are emphasised— perhaps an Islamic touch? The Italian artist, however, shows the dancers). The page on physical love *(cohitus)* is missing in the Viennese manuscript, having somehow been lost, but it is present in other manuscripts belonging to the same cultural ambiance, to which we refer briefly on page 136.

The nature of joy *est exitus virtutis et successive caliditatis*, is an outbreak of vital energy and the resulting heat. The best *ducit ad prosperitatem*, which we can take to mean "leads to feeling good." It is beneficial to sad people and *periclitantibus*, those who experience uncertainty because of danger. The harm that can result is surprising: *eo quod multiplicantur, mortem inducit*, repeated joy brings death. The remedy is to frequent wise men and this is a restatement of the old ethic of balancing the passions, a behavioral parallel of the medical principle of health as a balance of the humours. Perhaps the frequenting of wise men inspired the illustration in which an old man (Ellbochasim?) rests a paternal hand on the shoulder of a young girl, whose joy we are left to imagine.

ACTIVITY
Motus

Activity is essentially a progression of efforts *ad aliquem finem*, with some aim in mind, and the more noble the ends the better it is. The benefit lies in a harmonizing of the motor energy and the person who is moving. Activity becomes harmful when it is excessive. There are two ways to remedy this: by avoiding obstacles in one's course so that one's exertions are restricted to the right amount, or by desisting from the movement. *Motus fortis*, energetic activity, is suited to those with cold constitutions and *debilis*, or slow, moderate activity to people with hot constitutions.

CONTESTS
Luctatio

These can take many different forms depending on custom, as, for example, between young noblemen with swords and round shields. They benefit strong bodies that are not full of humours and the best contests are those *post cuius finem sentitur levitas*, at the end of which one feels light. One cannot define their specific nature as hot and cold or dry and moist, but they are suited to young people, to the springtime and its invigorating effect, and to those with hot and moist temperaments. They are not good for the chest and they may on some occasions result in the breaking of a vein. A bath and sleep afterwards are very helpful.

RIDING
Equitatio

Horse riding should give moderate movement and be practiced on flat ground with no obstacles, during a temperate season. It is preferable that one perspires. Its usefulness lies in raising the natural heat to a high point, stimulating the digestion, and diminishing the excess humours. Secondly, the pores are opened and the body's passages are cleansed by perspiration. Finally, it strengthens the limbs. It suits fully grown young people, and those with hot and moist temperaments. Too much riding can be harmful, and then one should rest and eat nourishing foods that partake of the moist.

HUNTING
Venatio terrestris

By hunting we mean hunting with dogs over crags and through woods, following the scent of and flushing out game as a pleasurable pursuit, more for diversion than from necessity. The natural effect on the body is cooling and drying, and for this reason it is very suitable for those with balanced temperaments and even more so for people with cold and moist ones whose excessive ardor and moisture are removed with this exercise. The humours become thinner, and the hunting of animals such as the hare is preferable as they are easy to find. Tired and dry after the hunt, one is revived by a bath and by oiling one's arms and legs. Young boys should not participate.

ANGER
Ira

Natura eius est ebulitio sanguinis circa cor propter appetitum vindicte, the essence or character of anger, so we read, is blood that boils around the heart from a desire for revenge. As regards health, anger relieves the distress of paralysis and its effects are appreciable: the blood is directed away from the heart to the body's extremities, the veins fill up, and lost color is restored. It is harmful to those who yield to illicit actions or impulses of the will. If repeated frequently, one's appearance turns yellow, and trembling, fever, and anxiety occur. Moral behavior and philosophical decorum will free one from anger.

SHYNESS
Verecondia

This is a natural process whereby heat withdraws inside, then returns to the outside, and when the second of these movements does not take place and the essential heat remains withdrawn, apprehension is created. Shyness is suited to those with temperate constitutions and to adolescence, but it is harmful to the vital force if it arises *ex malo furore*, from a wicked rage. One can throw off the harmful effects by a restorative action of discretion and reason, philosophy being the medicine of the soul.

VOMITING
Vomitus

This restores one's health by cleansing the stomach of matter that has no food value. It helps the overly full stomach and the upper parts of the body, and it is best when it happens easily to the broad-chested. It harms the eyes and stomach and constricts the chest. It helps to cover the eyes of the sufferer and adopt other appropriate remedies.

DRUNKENNESS
Ebrietas

This is mainly caused by excessive and inopportune drinking of wine which, because of its nature, disrupts the senses and *ystrumenta sensuum*, sensory organs. It is good for intense pain and against the deterioration of the humours. It is eminently suited to the very elderly and to those with cold constitutions when the rigors of winter set in. The harm that results is a heaviness of the brain. The cure is to vomit and take nourishment that comforts the brain.

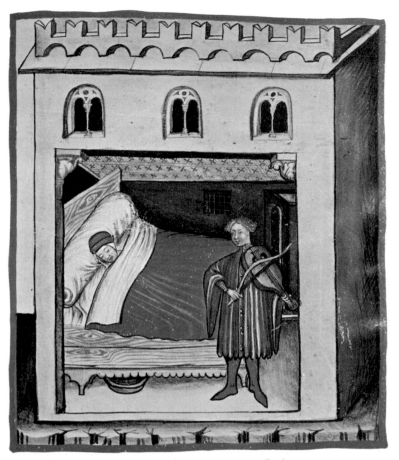

SLEEP
Sompnus

TALKING IN ONE'S SLEEP
Confabulationes in sompnis

We sleep for eight hours. Sleep is the immobility of the senses which warms and moistens to a moderate degree, fortifies the senses and body, and helps to digest food. The great Hippocrates says, "The sleeping body does not feel, but the soul stands watch, knows, sees the visible, hears the audible, moves, touches, grieves. . . ." Too much sleep is harmful; it *exicat corpus et resolvit virtutes*, dries out the body and dissipates the strength, principally because the stomach remains empty. Avoid sleeping during the daytime, which is always bad and worse on very hot days.

Talking in one's sleep occurs at every age, season, and climate, to people of every sort of constitution so that it is impossible to say to whom and when it is more suited. Its nature is double-sided: *rumor versus aut falsus*, what one says in one's sleep may be true or false. The very fact of talking in one's sleep generates more sleep and can be useful for this purpose. It is preferable to say things *convenientiores ad audiendum*, that are pleasant to hear because rude remarks are harmful, and it is fitting to pass from disagreeable to more pleasant subjects.

THE EVENING CONVERSATIONALIST
Confabulator

Sleep is nourished by evening conversation: *confabulatio natura est una causarum sompni*, conversation is by its nature one of the causes of sleep. The companion with whom one wishes to exchange some words should therefore be suitable to the mood of the person wanting to embrace sleep. It will be beneficial if the conversation is pleasurable, as it will improve the digestion, the senses, and the soul. It is annoying and harmful to listen to several persons talking when one would rather listen to only one. One must therefore impose silence on all the others. Evening conversation is suitable for everyone, except young children.

WAKEFULNESS
Vigilie

Its nature is an exercising of the senses which become hot and then dry; it is brought on by excess heat in the brain and causes mental anguish and indigestion if it is immoderate. As it is an intensified state of the mind, it can be useful *ad inquisitionem eorum quae sunt ad vitam*, for examining carefully what is of vital importance. The harm that it causes becomes evident when wakefulness is excessive: it tires the senses, dries the body, fills the head with vapors, leaves circles under the eyes, and excites anger. The remedy is sleep to be brought on by *olbis humectantibus*, nutritious fluids.

SINGING WITH ORGAN MUSIC AND STRINGS.
Organare cantum vel sonare

SINGING
Cantus

Singing consists of harmonizing the voices with the instruments, which are not, however, being played. The best singing is that which *allicit animos audientium*, engages the hearts of the listeners. It keeps away illness, but becoming accustomed to its pleasure is harmful for the very reason that it is too enjoyable; hence one must know how to practice it in moderation or abstain. Like few other things, it is suitable for everyone, in every region and season of the year.

Inducit delectationem, quando cantat suaviter, it is pleasurable when the sound is sweet. But this means that the accompaniment must harmonize with the voices. When, on the other hand, the singing is too subdued and out of tune, it is irritating. A gentleman must therefore have among his servants well-prepared musicians who know how to play a melody harmoniously. The entertainment is such that it is suitable for everyone, whatever their age or constitution.

DANCING TO MUSIC
Sonare et balare

"*Exercising the mind is not to be despised, for just as the body is made robust through exercise, the mind is nourished and invigorated through study. By exercising the mind, many have been freed from very great infirmities. Meditations, and singing of psalms with musical instruments, and listening to theological history are mental exercises which, by giving pleasure to the mind, nourish it so that all the faculties become stronger in resisting infirmities and overcoming them; and when in due course these exertions are made at the right time—after a perfect concoction (digestion) of food—they feed and fortify the mind and perfect the memory. Thence come gifted men fit to govern the republics. . . ."*

Castor Durante da Gualdo
A Treasury of Health, 1586

The feet and the body are required to move in time to the music: this should suffice to describe its nature. A dance must be chosen that is appropriate to the music and the movement of the person. Its usefulness lies in the fact that it partakes of the pleasure of harmonious agreement between the visible and the audible. When the dancer ceases to harmonize with the music, *fastidium facit*, it is annoying, and therefore one must regain that harmony. It is suited to most people of any age, except for young children.

The Book of the Cerruti Family:
From the Medicine of Hippocrates to the Fourteenth-Century Courts of the Po Valley

Towards the end of the last century, in 1895 to be precise, the great Austrian art historian Julius von Schlosser, who was later to write the famous *Kunstliteratur*, *(Literature of the Arts)*, under the name of Schlosser-Magnino—the second name came from his Italian mother—made known in an article in a magazine, which had proposed to illustrate the works of art owned by the Hapsburg royal family, a late medieval, illuminated manuscript that was none other than the work on which this book is based. Publishing some of the illustrations, Schlosser dwelt on the armorial bearing, printed on the first page, which he believed belonged to the Cerruti family of Verona. There are two escutcheons, for purposes of symmetry, supported by two dogs contra-rampant, displaying three gold disks on an azure field. The two surmounting crests terminate in a ram's head on the left and a spurred leg on the right. The dogs hold in their paws the hoists of standards bearing a red cross on a white field. In line with his identification of the owners of the coat of arms, which he believed to belong to the person who commissioned the manuscript, Schlosser attributed the illuminations to the School of Verona.

Although the manuscript, consisting of 108 pages or sheets, only slightly larger than the palm of one's hand, with 208 miniatures, continues to be known as *The Four Seasons of the House of Cerruti*, the theory as to the person who commissioned the work soon raised serious doubts. The oldest known coat of arms of the Cerruti family is to be found on a sixteenth-century tombstone and shows three wheels. The gold disks in the illustration seem rather like round-toothed shields; the standard with a red cross on a white field, which ought to have been the city's flag before the Venetian conquest, does not ever appear to have been used in Verona.

Leafing through the manuscript, which was written in Latin, one is immediately struck by certain Eastern references. As was already mentioned, the teacher in his chair (page 4) has been identified as the Arab doctor Ellbochasim de Baldach (Ibn Botlan); in two illustrations *(Nux indie e Ventus orientalis*, pages 76 and 10) we see people wearing Eastern-style clothes compared with the rest, who provide a detailed picture of Western dress in the late fourteenth century; the mention of dates, camel and gazelle meat, and soured milk refers to customs from the Arab world; and the text has a few words derived from Arabic, like *rusuri* and *rutab* for dates, *mesch* for vetchling, *savich* for creamy soup, *trij* for noodles.

As stated in the introduction, the text of the manuscript is a treatment, or resumé, of an Arabic compendium, the *Taqwim as-sihha* of Ibn Botlan. Not very much is known about this person. He was baptized a Christian with the name of Giovanni and he died in a monastery at Antioch in 1068 or later. He studied with a famous Arab doctor in Baghdad, practiced his skills in Mosul, Aleppo, Constantinople, and Egypt, and wrote on medicine and perhaps on theology as well. It was a great epoch for Arab medicine. Almost contemporaneous with Ibn Botlan is, for example, the Persian Avicenna (d. 1037), author of the *Canon (al-Qanum)*, which codified the medical principles of Hippocrates and Galen and the biology of Aristotle and served for centuries as a textbook for the medical schools of Western universities.

Taqwim as-sihha is an example, though a modest one, of the great historical function of Islamic culture: the passing on of classical culture to the medieval Western world, which had to a great extent lost it. It is a practical and curious work, a reference book that lists fruit trees, vegetables, spices, flowers, cereals and the foods derived from them, legumes, tubers, milk and milk products, salt, bread, fowl, meat from wild and domestic animals, the various parts of animals, wine and water, clothes, the four winds, the four seasons, states of mind, activities and pastimes. For each one of these items it gives in tabular form the same basic information relating to health. Given this tabular form of presentation, it was suggested that the Arabic title should not be translated "Notebook of Health" (the Italian word *taccuino*, which means notebook, is directly derived from *taqwim*, but has taken on its present meaning), but more properly *Tables of Health*.

We have indicated in the preceding pages the kind of information that Ibn Botlan gave his readers. It is interesting to see an entry in its entirety from the Latin translation of *The Four Seasons of the House of Cerruti*. For licorice the text reads:

Liquiritia: complexio calida et humida temperate.
Electio: recens, cuius radix media inter grossam et subtilem, lenis, equalis substantie.
Iu vamentum: confert raucedinis vocis es asperitati gutturis et provocat urinam, aperit opilationes nutritivorum et renum.
Nocumentum: eius sucus facit abominationem et debilitat apetitum.
Remotio nocumenti: cum passulis.
Quid generat: bonum sanguinem.
Convenit omnibus complexionibus, omni etati, tempore et regione.

Translated as faithfully as possible, this reads:

Licorice: constitution (or nature) moderately hot and moist.
What to choose (or what is preferable): recently picked, average-sized root between thick and thin, tender, even-textured.
Benefit: it is good for hoarseness and a sore throat and it makes one pass water, and it opens obstructions of the intestines and kidneys.
Harm: the juice causes nausea and weakens the appetite.
Remedy for the harm: raisins.
It generates: good blood.
It suits all constitutions (or temperaments), ages, times (seasons), and regions.

This information, which is arranged in seven categories (*Complexio, electio, iuvamentum, nocumentum, remotio nocumenti, quid generat, convenit*) is scrupulously given for each item, even, in one case, with a certain embarrassment. Regarding candles—these, too, are discussed in this universal reference book—it says of their nature *quae sunt de cera, sunt ex re calidori quam ille de sepo, non tamen debent graduari in complexione, inquantum sunt candele* (for this reason the wax ones are warmer than the tallow ones, but their constitution does not need to be graded; that is, the degree of their nature does not have to be given, because they are candles.)

There are in existence various manuscripts of the Latin translation of Ibn Botlan's reference book. Exactly when the translation was done or who did it is not verifiable. It is conceivable that more than one translation was done and various theories have been advanced. One translation may have been done about a hundred years after the death of Ibn Botlan by Gherardo da Cremona, a prolific medieval translator of Arabic works, who went to Toledo to study Ptolemy's *Almagest*, which he rendered into Latin from the Arabic (1175), together with some seventy other works on astronomy, astrology, arithmetic, algebra, geometry, geomancy, philosophy, and medicine, some works by Ptolemy in Greek, and original Arabic works, such as those of Avicenna. During the preceding century the city of Toledo, under Arab rule since 711, had been conquered in May 1085 by Alphonso VI, king of Leon and Castile, who made it his capital. Another translator, perhaps the first, was the Jew Faradj ben Salem (in Latin Farraghutus), who was at the Neapolitan court of Charles d'Anjou towards the end of the thirteenth century. It is interesting that a manuscript with Farraghutus's translation of Ibn Botlan, now in the Bibliothèque Nationale of Paris, is identified as a manuscript mentioned in the inventory of the library at Pavia of the Viscontis, dukes of Milan, part of which was taken to France by Louis XII after his brief conquest of Milan. This establishes a link between the Arab doctor from Baghdad and the region of the Po where the type of work, of which *The Book of the Cerruti Family* is not an isolated example, originated during the late Middle Ages.

Before going into the question of iconography, we should first look at the sources of Ibn Botlan, that body of knowledge and doctrines that provided the basis for his book. In the introduction we noted that the medicine of Hippocrates was the principal source, and we can supplement this with a few details. In the fifth century B.C. a younger contemporary of Pythagoras, the physician Alcmaeon, lived in Croton. His work *De Natura* has been lost and traces of it remain only in the works of later authors. He believed that "health and illness depend on pairs of contrasting elements like hot and cold, moisture and dryness, bitter and sweet, and so forth" (R. Margotta), an idea that was to take hold. Living at approximately the same time was Empedocles of Agrigento (483–423 B.C.), philosopher, physician, poet, and orator who, legend says, threw himself into the crater of Mount Etna to make people believe that he had been taken up among the gods. Etna apparently regurgitated one of his bronze sandals, thereby dispelling any mystery about his disappearance.

In reality Empedocles left his country because of dissension and died in the Peloponnese. He was the first to formulate the theory of the four "origins" of all things, the four primary elements: fire, air, earth, and water. Hippocrates was about twenty years his junior. Born on the Aegean island of Kos in 460, he travelled widely and died in Thessaly, possibly a centenarian plus. The natural philosophy of Hippocrates is the same as that of Empedocles, which says that the human body is formed by the union of the four elements and by the qualities of each one of them: the cold, the hot, the dry, and the moist. In one of his books, *Concerning the Nature of Man*, Hippocrates wrote, "The human body contains within it blood, phlegm, yellow bile, and black bile. They constitute the body's nature and create illness and health. We are healthy when these humours combine in a mixture *(crasis)* that has the right strength and quantities; then the blending is perfect. We are ill when one of the humours is deficient or in excess, or has failed to combine with the others. When one of the humours becomes separated and isolated in the body, not only does the vacated place become ill, but the newly occupied place becomes blocked up and illness and pain result."

Of the four humours we do not need to define blood and bile (yellow). Black bile, or melancholy, does not have a corresponding substance in the organic makeup of the human body. Phlegm, however, according to the ancients, is represented by nasal mucus, bronchial and intestinal catarrh, and other mucosal secretions.

This is Hippocrates's theory of the pathology of the humours. "Anyone today who considers this an eccentric theory of pathology, based on the harmonies and disharmonies of the humours," we read in a history of medicine, "should know that it was still considered valid in the first half of the nineteenth century."

Four elements, four qualities, four humours—the analogies are extended, as seen in the diagram on page 139, to the temperaments, or constitutions (phlegmatic, sanguine, bilious, melancholic), the ages of man, the seasons, and the cardinal points. These are the medical, biological, and naturalistic concepts that were passed on to the Arabs. This occurred, on at least one occasion, because of a matter of heresy. Nestorius, the patriarch of Constantinople, came into conflict with the monks and the people in 428 A.D. when he rejected the designation of "*Theotokos*," or "Mother of God," for the Virgin. At the Council of Ephesus in 431 Saint Cyril of Alexandria denounced the teachings of Nestorius. His followers, the Nestorian heretics, founded a medical school at Edessa (the modern Urfa in Turkey); but in 489 the bishop Cyrus obtained permission from the emperor Zeno to close the school and expel the instructors. They took refuge in Persia, where they established a thriving medical school at Gundeshapur. Much later, after the Arab conquest, the school at Gundeshapur became the cradle of Islamic medicine.

A classical text that the Arabs valued greatly is *De Materia Medica*, written in Greek by Pedanius Dioscorides. It is said that a Byzantine emperor was amazed to discover that the finest present he could offer to a Muslim military leader was a copy of this work by Dioscorides. Born in Cilicia,

Dioscorides was a skillful military surgeon at the time of the emperor Nero, as well as an amateur botanist. The five volumes of his *De Materia Medica* deal with herbs and spices, ointments and oils, foods of animal and vegetable origin, plants and roots, wines and pharmaceutical remedies derived from minerals.

There is an unmistakable affinity with the material of Ibn Botlan's compendium. A Viennese manuscript of Dioscorides's work, dated 512 A.D., is the oldest of the herbals in existence. The tradition of the medieval herbals, which is broadly linked with the ancient or Arabic illustration of Dioscorides's work, helped to shape the iconography of the late medieval notebooks on health.

Starting from Hippocrates's theory of medicine and Empedocles's philosophy of nature, the science of food and ancient pharmacopoeia was developed according to a very logical system: everything being composed of a different combination of the four basic elements has a pair of qualities with one or another element predominating. Basil, for example, is hot and dry, pears are cold and moist, partridge is hot and moist, like noodles, and so forth. The action of different substances can be deduced by keeping in mind the diagram of harmonies according to the principle *contraria contrariis:* a hot thing is effective against a prevailing cold and wet humour, and so forth. The degree of efficacy depends on the degree of intensity with which the thing possesses the quality. Hence the advantages of classifying the qualities of individual things along a uniform scale.

This was the work of Arabic medicine (there are four degrees). Identification of the nature of different things "was very often arbitrary or based solely on the more apparent rather than real features" and from this "was derived the heating or cooling, drying or moistening action exerted by the various agents on the organism" (S. Baglioni).

A glance at the chart on the following pages, giving all the subject matter illustrated in *The Book of the Cerruti Family* with the qualities and degree which the text, derived from Ibn Botlan, attributed to them, may lead to some surprising observations.

We have mentioned that there is more than one illuminated *tacuinum* like the one that possibly belonged to the Cerruti family of Verona. After Schlosser's findings, a French scholar pointed out the existence of a similar manuscript in the Bibliothèque Nationale in Paris. Less than a decade later a third manuscript was found, preserved in the Biblioteca Casanatense in Rome. The text of the three manuscripts appeared to be more or less the same. Ellbochasim de Baldach became Albukasem de Baldac in the Paris manuscript and Ububchasym de Baldach in the Rome one; the subject matter was the same with a few variations; and the iconography of all three belonged to the Po Valley version of the international Gothic style of the second half of the fourteenth century.

What had happened was this: someone had decided—at that time a work of this kind could only have originated as the result of a commission, which came exclusively from the aristocratic ambiance of the courts—that Ibn Botlan's reference book on health and hygiene, which was already in cir-

culation (that is, there were some manuscript copies in the libraries of ruling princes, or monasteries, or scholars), should be turned into an illustrated book that would delight the eye as well as nourish the mind. We could go so far as to draw an analogy with the *Book of Hours*, the illustrated book of prayers that a nobleman had caused to be illuminated. It served to comfort the mind, whereas the *Tacuinum sanitatis* was devised to comfort the body. The analogy can be taken further if we take into account that the illustrations of the *Book of Hours* deal largely with the profane side of life. And the *tacuini* go one step further by presenting fresh, almost gossipy pictures of the life and customs of that time, when the art of illumination met an innate need for images, and the visual pleasure it provided was not unlike that of photography and television today. That this study of life should be conducted on a plane of joyous escapism, of aristocratic or, if you like, literary detachment, is not surprising when we recall the courtly ambiance for which it was destined.

This is not the place to discuss the details of the controversy that has been going on among scholars over the past decades since the discovery of these manuscripts, but it may be useful to conclude these comments with the current findings given in a stimulating essay by Louisa Cogliati Arano. In summing up the theories and verified facts, she considers the three abovementioned manuscripts along with a few others, looks at the chronological sequence, and traces them back to a single formative source, the artistic culture and activity of Giovannino de' Grassi, originator of the oldest manuscript, to which he personally put his hand in part, and producer, directly or indirectly, through the colleagues and assistants of his atelier, of the other manuscripts. Giovanni de' Grassi is, as we know, one of the principal masters of the international Gothic style and one of the most eminent personalities of Milanese art of his time, which is also that of Duke Gian Galeazzo Visconti.

Architect, painter, sculptor, and illuminator—the complete artist—Giovanni de' Grassi was born around 1340 and died in 1398. He is the author of the distinguished book of drawings in the Biblioteca Civica of Bergamo and was active in the building of Milan Cathedral. His name appears in the records after 1391 with the designation "architect in charge."

The first of the *tacuini*, according to Louisa Cogliati Arano, is neither of the aforementioned three manuscripts but one in pen and sepia ink that is preserved in the University Library in Liège. Only the first few pages have been colored. It was probably begun around 1380 and it confirms "what must have been the practice of Giovannino: to give thorough instructions for carrying out a work and then entrust a good part of the execution to the atelier" (L. Cogliati Arano). The work was possibly commissioned by a member of the Savoia family.

The second manuscript is thought to be the Paris one which belonged to Verde Visconti, a daughter of Bernabò, married to Leopold of Austria in 1365. The third is *The Book of the Cerruti Family*, and the fourth is the Casanatense manuscript, which probably dates from the last years of the fourteenth century.

The manuscript that has been the subject of this book bears another coat of arms, along with the one attributed to the Cerrutis, which, after Schlosser's publication, was identified as belonging to George of Liechtenstein, bishop of Trento from 1390 to 1407 when he left the city. It was he who commissioned the frescos for the room called "The Eagle's Tower" in the Buonconsiglio castle (1400–07), frescos that display much the same mood as that of the manuscript's illuminations. Similar clues and others lead Louisa Cogliati Arano to conclude that there may be some substance to the theory that "The manuscript could have been executed for the same George of Liechtenstein when he became bishop, hence immediately after 1390. It is highly probable that the bishop turned to an artist employed by the Visconti and Della Scala families. It is tempting to suggest that his desire to acquire this type of work was stimulated by his knowledge of the valuable *Tacuinum* owned by Verde Visconti, wife of Duke Leopold of Austria."

In 1407 the bishop was driven from Trento and in 1410 the city was taken by Frederick of the Tyrol. In his inventory he refers to a *herbalarium cum figuris pictis* which must be our *Tacuinum*. In the course of dynastic upheavals the manuscript passed from the castle at Innsbruck to the library of the castle at Ambras, then to Vienna (1806) in the imperial historical-artistic collections, which have been kept in the Kunsthistorisches Museum since 1881. In 1936 it was acquired by the Oesterreichische Nationalbibliothek, where it is still to be found today with the pressmark *Codex Vindobonensis Series Nova, 2644.*

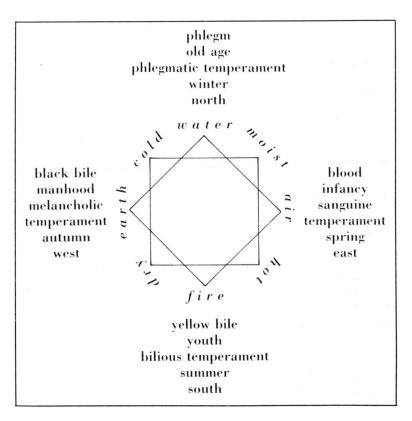

Diagram of the harmonious relationships among the four elements—earth, water, air, fire—with their "qualities" (cold, moist, hot, dry) and with humors, ages of man, temperaments, seasons, and cardinal points, in accordance with the principles of ancient medicine.

The Qualities of Things According to
The Four Seasons of the House of Cerruti

According to the natural philosophy of Empedocles and the medical teachings of Hippocrates, the four basic qualities of dry, cold, hot, and moist—corresponding to the four elements of land, air, fire, and water—are to be found in every entity in the cosmos. Everything in the vegetable, mineral, and animal world partakes of two of these qualities, such as, of the hot and dry, or cold and moist. Each of these qualities enjoys, according to a later theory developed by Arab physicians, one of four possible degrees of intensity. A substance may, for example, be hot in the first, second, third, or fourth degree. This table shows the nature *(complexio)* and degree of the single things as defined by Ellbochasim de Baldach in the *Tacuinum sanitatis* of the Vienna manuscript. The qualities of each item are indicated in the appropriate column by the presence of a dot or a number. The number, indicating the degree, is given only when the text supplies it, which it does not always do.

SUBJECT	HOT	COLD	MOIST	DRY
Acorns			2	
Almonds	2			2
Almond Oil	2		1	
Alum Water	3			3
Ambergris	2			2
Anise	3			3
Apples				2
Apricots		2	2	
Asparagus	1		1	
Aubergine	4			3
Autumn		2		
Bananas	2		1	
Barley		2		2
Barley Water		2		2
Basil	1			2
Basil Ocymum	2			1
Bay Tree Berries	3			3
Beans	1		1	
Beetroot	1			1
Bitter Oranges		•	•	
Black Bread	2			
Black Cherries		3		2
Black Olives				•
Boiled Wheat			2	2
Brains		2	2	
Bran Bread	2			

SUBJECT	HOT	COLD	MOIST	DRY
Broad Beans		1		2
Butter	•		•	
Cabbages	1			2
Calf's Head	2		2	
Camphor		3		3
Cane Sugar	•		•	
Capers	2			
Carob Beans	1			2
Castrated Animals		•		
Celery	1		1	
Cherries		2	3	
Chestnuts	1			2
Chick-Peas		2	2	
Citrine Wine	2			2
Citrons		2		3
Cow and Camel Meat	2			2
Crane	2			2
Cream of Barley Soup		2		2
Cucumbers		2	2	
Dates	2		2	
Dates, sweet	1			2
Dates, wild		1		2
Dill	2–3			2–3
Dried and Salt Meat	2			3
Dried Figs	1			1
Ducks and Geese	2		2	

SUBJECT	HOT	COLD	MOIST	DRY
East Wind	2			
Eyes	2		2	
Fat and Lard	2		2	
Fennel	3			2
Figs	1		1	
Fish		3	3	
Fresh Cheese			•	•
Galingale	3			2
Garlic	4			3
Gazelle	2			2
Gelatin			•	•
Goose Eggs	•			
Grapes	1			2
Hare	2			2
Hazelnuts	1			
Heart	2			2
Hens' Eggs (white)			•	•
Hens' Eggs (yolk)	•		•	
Honey	2			2
Horehound	3			3
Horseradish	3			2
Hot Water	2	2		
Hyssop	3			3
Inulin	3		2	
Italian Millet			1	2
Jujubes	1		1	

SUBJECT	HOT	COLD	MOIST	DRY
Junket			●	●
Kid	1		1	
Lamprey		2	2	
Leeks	3			2
Lemons		2		3
Lettuce		2	2	
Lily	2			3
Linen Clothes		2		2
Licorice	●		●	
Liver	2		2	
Lupines	2			2
Mandrake		3		2
Marjoram	3			3
Matured Cheese		●		●
Medlars		2		2
Melons		2	3	
Milk	●			
Millet		1		2
Millet Bread		2		2
Mint	3			3
Mountain Celery	2			2
Musk	2			2
Mustard	3			3
Mutton	2		2	
North Wind		3		2
Nutmeg	2		1	
Old Aromatic Wine	2			3
Olive Oil (black)	●		●	
Olive Oil (green)		●		●
Onions	4		3	
Parsley	2			2
Parsnips	2		1	
Partridge	2		2	
Partridge Eggs	●			
Peaches		2	3	
Peacocks	2		2	
Pears		1		2

SUBJECT	HOT	COLD	MOIST	DRY
Pellitory	1			1
Pheasants	2		2	
Pickled Fish		2		2
Pigeons	●		●	
Pine Nuts	2			1
Plums		1	2	
Pork		1	2–3	
Prawns		2	1	
Pumpkins		2	2	
Quail	●		●	
Quinces		2		2
Rainwater		4	4	
Raisins	1		1	
Rice		2		2
Ricotta		●	●	
Roast Meats	●			●
Robust Red Wine	2			2
Rocket and Watercress	1		1	
Roosters	2			2
Roses		1		3
Rose Water	●			●
Rue	3			3
Rye		2		2
Saffron	1			1
Sage	1			2
Salt	2			3
Salt Water	2			2
Salted Fish	2			2
Silk Clothes	2			2
Small Birds and Thrushes	2		2	
Snow and Ice		3	3	
Sorghum	1			1
Sour Apples		2		2
Sour Milk		●	●	
Sour Pomegranates		2	1	
South Wind	2		1	

SUBJECT	HOT	COLD	MOIST	DRY
Spelt	●			
Spinach		1	1	
Spleen	2			2
Spring	2		2	
Spring Water		4	4	
Starch		2		2
Sugar	1		2	
Summer	3			2
Swedes	1		2	
Sweet Pomegranates	1		2	
Sycamore		2		2
Syrup of Vinegar	●	●		
Tagliatelle (Noodles)	2		2	
Testicles	2		2	
Theriaca	●			●
Tripe		2		2
Truffles		2	2	
Turnip	1		2–3	
Turtledoves	2		2	
Udder	2		2	
Unleavened Bread		2		
Veal	1		1	
Verjuice		3		2
Vetchling	2		2	
Vinegar		1		3
Violets		1	2	
Walnuts	1			2
Watermelon		2	2	
Watermelons from East	2		2	
West Wind				2
Wheat	2		2	
White Wine	2			2
Winter		3	2	
Woolen Clothes	2			2
Wormwood	1–2			2

Index